2-INGREDIENT
MIRACLE DOUGH
COOKBOOK

EASY LOWER-CARB RECIPES FOR FLATBREADS, BAGELS, DESSERTS AND MORE

ERIN RENOUF MYLROIE

PAGE STREET
PUBLISHING CO.

PAGE STREET
PUBLISHING CO.

First published in 2019 by

Page Street Publishing Co.

27 Congress Street, Suite 105

Salem, MA 01970

www.pagestreetpublishing.com

Distributed by Macmillan, sales in Canada by The Canadian Manda Group.

23 22 21 20 19   1 2 3 4 5

ISBN-13: 978-1-62414-744-9

ISBN-10: 1-62414-744-5

Library of Congress Control Number: 2018958701

Cover and book design by Meghan Baskis for Page Street Publishing Co.

Photography by Ken Goodman

Printed and bound in the United States

TO THOSE WHO KNOW I LOVE THEM WITHOUT
REQUIRING ANY MENTION WHATSOEVER,
BUT ESPECIALLY TO MY MOTHER, WHO ALWAYS
SEES MY PATH BEFORE I DO.

INTRODUCTION   **7**

MASTER RECIPE WITH VEGAN AND GLUTEN-FREE OPTIONS   9

Basic Bagels with Master Recipe   10

Make Your Own Self-Rising Flour   11

BREADS, ROLLS, BAGELS AND BUNS   13

Double Everything Bagels   14

Cinnamon-Raisin-Walnut Bagels with Honey-Walnut Cream Cheese   17

Garlic and Cheddar Bagel Twists   18

Triple Onion Cream Cheese–Stuffed Bagel Balls   21

Sun-Dried Tomato Pesto Cream Cheese–Stuffed Bagel Balls   22

Cheddar, Onion and Black Pepper Visiting Loaf   25

Pita Pockets with Cucumber Raita   26

Israeli Sesame Ring Bread with Salt and Herbs for Dipping   29

Rustic Olive, Feta and Roasted Red Pepper Loaf   30

Red Onion and Gruyère Fougasse   33

Monterey Jack Cheese, Dill and Scallion Biscuits   34

Cheddar and Old Bay Butter-Topped Drop Biscuits   37

Poppy Seed Hamburger Buns   38

German Seeded Rye Rolls   41

Irish Dilly-Rye Loaf   42

Soft and Buttery Dinner Rolls   45

Pesto-Parmesan Twists   46

Spicy Pepper Jack Jalapeño Roll-Ups   49

Buttery Honey Dijon–Glazed Soft Pretzels   50

Pretzel Bites with Sweet and Tangy Cheese Sauce   53

Giant Cream Cheese and Jalapeño–Stuffed Pretzel for a Crowd   54

Buttery Parmesan and Garlic Knots   57

Bacon, Fig and Gruyère Volcano Rolls   58

FLATBREADS, PIZZAS AND MAIN DISH BREADS 61

Caramelized Onion, Asiago and Rosemary Focaccia 62

Spinach, Feta and Red Bell Pepper
Breakfast Flatbreads 65

Maple Bacon, Jalapeño and Gruyère
Good Morning Flatbreads 66

Super-Food Crispy Kale, Avocado and
Frizzled Egg Flatbreads 69

Spicy Italian Sausage and Mozzarella Calzones 70

Denver Ham and Cheddar Breakfast Pockets 73

Black Bean and Pepper Jack Baked
Huevos Rancheros 74

California Pizza with Fresh Greens, Olives
and Avocado 77

Grandma's Long Island Tomato and Herb Pizza 78

Four Seasons Sheet Pan Pizza—Pizza Quattro
Stagioni 81

Deep-Dish Chicago-Style Pizza 82

Golden Potato and Rosemary Pizza 85

30-Minute Start-to-Finish Pizza Margherita 86

Olive Oil, Tomato and Herb Pizza al Capriccio 89

Southern French Olive and Caper Pissaladière 90

Classic Sausage and Pepperoni Stromboli 93

Philadelphia Cheesesteak Stromboli 94

Chicken and Butternut Squash Potpie
with Sage-Herbed Crust 97

Chinese Bao with Plum Barbecue Chicken 98

Curried Potato and Pea Samosas 101

Three-Cheese Empanadas 102

Chilean-Style Cumin-Scented Beef Empanadas 105

Buffalo Chicken and Blue Cheese Pockets 106

Grilled Moroccan Chicken and
Vegetable Flatbread 109

Georgian Cheese and Egg Bread—Khachapuri 110

English Beef and Potato Hand Pie "Pasties" 113

Pizza Bianco-Style Fig, Prosciutto and
Cheese Sandwiches 114

Octoberfest Cheesy Mustard-Wrapped Brats 117

Texas Chorizo and Pickled Jalapeño Kolaches 118

Spinach, Gruyère and Bacon Quiche 121

SWEETS AND TREATS 123

Raspberry-Orange Breakfast Rolls 124

Maple-Pecan Sticky Buns 127

Cinnamon-Cardamom Braid 128

Lemon Cream Cheese Breakfast Pastries 131

French Toast Cinnamon and Maple Bites 132

Blueberry-Lemon Visiting Loaf 135

New York–Style Crumb Coffee Cake 136

Cini-Mini Churros with Milk Chocolate
Dipping Sauce 139

Lemon and Vanilla Italian Donuts—Castagnole 140

Raspberry-Filled Jelly Donut Holes 143

Sweet Irish Soda Bread with Currants and Raisins 144

Pineapple and Coconut Kolaches 147

Caramel-Apple Kuchen 148

Easy Liege-Style Waffles with Berries and
Belgian Chocolate 151

Juicy Blackberry Cobbler 152

Strawberry Twists with Lemonade Dipping Sauce 155

Strawberry Shortcakes with Cream Cheese Filling 156

Brown Sugar and Oatmeal Streusel–Topped
Blueberry Minicakes 159

Cranberry and Lemon Hot Cross Buns 160

Peach Beehives with Honey Butter 163

Orange Creamsicle Loaf Cake 164

Ginger and Brown Sugar Banana Cake 167

Fudgy Double Chocolate Snack Cake 168

ACKNOWLEDGMENTS 170

ABOUT THE AUTHOR 171

INDEX 172

INTRODUCTION

I can be a little skeptical; I confess. It took me a few times seeing "Two-Ingredient Dough" splashed around the Internet before I could warm up to the idea. I consider myself a pretty dedicated baker, one who thinks nothing of spending three days to create the perfect aged pizza dough, one who has worked for years on developing a perfect golden and crusty French baguette. The idea of a dough that could be ready in minutes with only two ingredients seemed almost like fool's gold, a little attention-grabbing and probably too good to be true. It was a hard sell for me.

Months later, as I was trying to clean out the fridge to leave on a family vacation, I noticed I had about a cupful of Greek yogurt at the bottom of the container. Ingredient number one was staring at me, begging to be used. I didn't have ingredient number two (self-rising flour), but a quick search on the Internet instructed me to make an easy substitute with pantry staples—just a cup of all-purpose flour, baking powder, a bit of baking soda and a little salt. I muttered to myself a little about it not going to be very good, but still I mixed up my dough, shaped it into four bagels and popped it into the oven.

Twenty minutes later, I repented of my non-believing ways and became fully indoctrinated in the miracle of two-ingredient dough. I've been on a mission since then, waving bagels and proclaiming the benefits of this fast and easy formula. Anyone who can hold a spoon can make two-ingredient dough. Everyone can remember the ingredient list: equal parts Greek yogurt and self-rising flour. There's no waiting, no rising, no complicated or fussy techniques here. It's just that easy.

But there's more to it than that. A quick word about health here. This dough is naturally lower in calories and carbohydrates, since half of the bulk of the dough comes from protein-rich Greek yogurt. You can use nonfat, low-fat or full-fat Greek yogurt in any of these recipes, so use the Greek yogurt that works best with your way of eating. I'm not a nutritionist, and I don't want to delve too deeply into science here, but if, like most Americans, you're trying to eat fewer calories and carbs, this dough can fit seamlessly into your healthy eating plan.

In fact, the dough can fit into just about any style of eating. Low-calorie or low-fat eating? You can make a fat-free bagel with just 150 calories using my master recipe. Vegan? Just swap out the Greek yogurt for a vegan variety of Greek yogurt. Gluten-free? Use a gluten-free flour blend. No refined grains? Simply make your own self-rising flour with any whole grain using the formula provided in my Master Recipe section (page 10). This dough does not discriminate. It will work for anyone.

And now, I've created dozens of mouth-watering recipes for you to enjoy, all starting with the simple formula of those two foundational ingredients: Greek yogurt and self-rising flour. You'll find a plethora of breads, pretzels and rolls, main dishes like cheesy pizzas and grilled chicken flatbreads and even some luxurious desserts, like Italian donuts and chocolate cake.

Two-ingredient dough might seem a little too good to be true, but that's the miracle. It's all good, no matter how you slice it.

Erin

MASTER RECIPE WITH VEGAN AND GLUTEN-FREE OPTIONS

This is the basic, miraculous TWO-INGREDIENT dough. Anyone can make it. Anyone can remember the ingredient list: self-rising flour and plain Greek yogurt. You can use nonfat, low-fat or full-fat yogurt, but DO make sure it's Greek yogurt. Use this Master Recipe to try out a few easy bagels or rolls. Once you see how easy it is to make delicious breads with two ingredients and very little work or patience, you'll be hooked.

BASIC BAGELS WITH MASTER RECIPE

MAKES 4

1 cup (120 g) self-rising flour (store-bought or homemade [see page 11])
1 cup (250 g) plain, nonfat, low-fat or full-fat Greek yogurt*

To make the dough, in a medium bowl, simply combine the flour and the yogurt by stirring with a wooden spoon until the mixture forms a shaggy ball. Set the wooden spoon aside and knead the mixture in the bowl by hand for about ten turns, or just until there are no dry spots in the dough. You can also generously flour a work surface and knead the dough on the surface, if you prefer. Gather the dough into a ball.

From this point, you can divide the dough into four equal sections. Shape each section into a ball and hold it in your hand. Push your thumb through the middle of the dough to form a center ring (just a standard bagel shape), about 1 inch (2.5 cm) in diameter. Alternatively, you can roll each section into a snake shape, about 8 inches (20 cm) long. Connect the ends and pinch them together to form a bagel shape. Place the shaped bagels on a parchment-lined baking sheet. Beat one egg** in a small bowl; brush the beaten egg onto the bagels in a thin coating. Sprinkle the bagels with Everything Bagel Seasoning (see note on page 14) or sesame seeds, if desired.

Bake the bagels at 425°F (220°C) for 16 to 18 minutes, or until the bagels are golden brown and spring back to the touch. Let the bagels cool for 5 minutes on the baking sheet. Remove the bagels from the baking sheet and enjoy warm, or cool completely and store in an airtight container for up to 2 days at room temperature or slice and freeze for up to 3 months.

*For vegan dough, substitute vegan-alternative Greek yogurt, such as Daiya.

**For vegan dough, omit the egg wash and brush with olive oil instead.

MAKE YOUR OWN SELF-RISING FLOUR

Self-rising flour is a mixture of flour, leavening and salt. Most of us don't keep it on hand, but the good news is that you don't need to. You can make your own quickly and easily. I rarely buy self-rising flour since it is much more expensive than all-purpose flour. You can double or triple this recipe and keep the extra self-rising flour on hand for convenience.

MAKES 1 CUP (120 G)

1 cup (120 g) all-purpose flour*
2 tsp (8 g) baking powder
¼ tsp baking soda
¾ tsp salt

In a small bowl, combine the flour, baking powder, soda and salt. Store in an airtight container or use immediately.

For gluten-free dough, create your own gluten-free self-rising flour. Use 1 cup (120 g) of gluten-free flour (recommended Bob's Gluten-Free Flour), plus 2 teaspoons (8 g) baking powder, ¼ teaspoon baking soda, and 1½ teaspoons (8 g) salt.

BREADS, ROLLS, BAGELS AND BUNS

Just think, in twenty or so minutes, you could be having fresh, warm bread with your family. You'll find round rustic loaves, pretzels, bagels, buns, rolls and all types of wonderful breads here that are a snap to prepare and delicious to eat. What are you waiting for? Go forth and bake!

DOUBLE EVERYTHING BAGELS

You are already know that "everything" bagels are good, but these are doubly good. They've got the "everything" flavor of minced onions, garlic, sesame seeds and poppy seeds on the inside as well as the outside. If you really love the Everything Bagel flavor—like I do—mix a tablespoon or two into a few ounces of softened cream cheese for your bagel schmear—now you've got a triple Everything Bagel. If you can't find Everything Bagel Seasoning, see my note below.

MAKES 4 BAGELS

1 cup (120 g) self-rising flour, plus more for kneading

1 cup (250 g) plain Greek yogurt

1 tbsp (10 g) Everything Bagel Seasoning (see note), plus a couple of tbsp (20 g) more for sprinkling on top

1 egg, beaten

Cream cheese, for serving, optional

Preheat the oven to 425°F (220°C). Line a baking sheet with parchment paper or foil and spray lightly with nonstick cooking spray and set it aside.

In a medium bowl, combine the self-rising flour, yogurt and 1 tablespoon (10 g) of the Everything Bagel Seasoning by stirring the dough with a wooden spoon until the mixture forms a shaggy ball. Set the wooden spoon aside and knead the mixture in the bowl by hand for about ten turns until the dough is well combined and no dry crumbs remain. Sprinkle in a little more flour if the dough remains sticky.

Gather the dough into a ball. Divide the dough into four equal sections, rolling each section into a smaller ball. Shape each ball into a bagel by either rolling it into a snake shape and joining the ends or by pushing your thumb through the center of the ball to create a hole in the dough for a bagel shape.

Dip or brush the top and sides of the bagels in the beaten egg. Sprinkle the bagels generously with the Everything Bagel Seasoning. Place the bagels on the prepared cookie sheet. Bake the bagels for 16 to 18 minutes, or until they are golden brown and very fragrant. Let the bagels cool for about 10 minutes on the baking sheet. Serve them warm and fresh with a schmear of cream cheese, or cool them completely and toast them up.

NOTE: If you aren't able to find Everything Bagel Seasoning, you can make your own by combining the following ingredients that are widely available in the spice section of grocery stores: 1 tablespoon (12 g) of minced onions, 1 tablespoon (10 g) of minced garlic, 1 tablespoon (10 g) of sesame seeds, 1 tablespoon (9 g) of poppy seeds and a teaspoon of kosher salt. Store in an airtight container.

CINNAMON-RAISIN-WALNUT BAGELS WITH HONEY-WALNUT CREAM CHEESE

I don't usually want raisins in my baked goods, but I make an exception for a cinnamon-raisin bagel. If you're opposed to raisins, you can use dried cranberries, but you might as well give raisins one more try. C'mon. (My little sister made me try a raisin bagel in New York, and now I'm a raisin-bagel convert. You might like it too?) The raisins just add the perfect little bit of fruity sweetness against that heady cinnamon. Even better—if you're talking about a cinnamon-raisin bagel with a schmear (or more) of dreamy honey-walnut cream cheese, then I'm all in.

MAKES 4 BAGELS

BAGELS

¼ cup (40 g) raisins or dried cranberries

¼ cup (60 ml) boiling water

1 cup (120 g) self-rising flour

1 cup (250 g) plain Greek yogurt

1 tbsp (13 g) sugar, plus more for sprinkling on top, optional

1 tsp cinnamon, plus more for garnish, optional

¼ cup (30 g) chopped walnuts

1 egg, beaten

HONEY-WALNUT CREAM CHEESE

4 oz (115 g) cream cheese, softened

2 tbsp (45 g) honey

2 tbsp (15 g) chopped walnuts

A pinch of ground cinnamon

Preheat the oven to 425°F (220°C). Line a baking sheet with parchment paper and set aside.

Place the raisins in a small bowl and cover them with boiling water for a few minutes to soften them up. Set the raisins aside while you prepare the dough.

For the bagels, in a medium bowl, combine the flour, yogurt, sugar and cinnamon with a wooden spoon until the mixture forms a shaggy ball. Drain off and discard the excess water on the raisins and add the raisins to the dough along with the walnuts. Set your spoon aside and use your hand to knead the dough in the bowl for 1 minute, or until the dough forms a smooth ball. Divide the dough into four somewhat equal sections.

Shape each section into a bagel by rolling into an 8-inch (20-cm) snake shape and pinching into a bagel shape or by forming each dough section into a ball and pushing your thumb through the bottom to create the bagel shape.

Place the bagels on the prepared baking sheet and brush them lightly with the beaten egg. Sprinkle with additional cinnamon and sugar, if you like. Bake for 16 to 18 minutes, or until they are golden brown. Let the bagels cool on the baking sheet for 10 minutes before serving.

For the honey-walnut cream cheese, in a small bowl, combine the cream cheese and honey until smooth and creamy. Stir in the walnuts and cinnamon.

Top the bagels with cinnamon and sugar, if using. Serve the bagels with a generous schmear of Honey-Walnut Cream Cheese. Heavenly!

GARLIC AND CHEDDAR BAGEL TWISTS

These are one of my family's favorite treats at a popular theme park in southern California. It was that captivating scent of warm fresh bread and garlic that drew us all in, but it's the pockets of melted cheddar in the dough that keeps us coming back for more. It's been fun to be able to bring a little magic home by making these in our kitchen.

MAKES 2 BIG TWISTS

1 cup (120 g) self-rising flour, plus more for work surface

1 cup (250 g) plain Greek yogurt

2 tsp (7 g) minced garlic

¾ cup (95 g) shredded sharp cheddar

1 tsp poppy seeds, plus more for sprinkling on top

1 tbsp (15 ml) butter, melted

Preheat the oven to 425°F (220°C) and line a baking sheet with a sheet of parchment paper.

In a medium bowl, using a wooden spoon, combine the flour and yogurt until a shaggy dough ball forms. Knead the mixture with your hand a few times until the dough develops into a smooth ball.

Generously flour a work surface. Transfer the dough to the work surface and gently roll or press the dough into a 12 x 6-inch (30 x 15–cm) rectangle, sprinkling more flour in as needed to prevent sticking. Sprinkle the dough with the garlic, cheddar and poppy seeds. Starting with the long edge, roll the dough into a cylinder, pinching the edges shut. Using a sharp knife or scissors, cut the dough in half lengthwise.

Transfer the dough halves to a cutting board. Twist each half four times each. Brush the dough lightly with some of the butter and sprinkle with some poppy seeds. Bake for 20 to 22 minutes, or until they are golden brown and very fragrant. Brush the dough with the remaining butter and serve nice and warm with a big napkin.

TRIPLE ONION CREAM CHEESE–STUFFED BAGEL BALLS

There's a popular bagel joint in NYC that stuffs cream cheese into little bagel balls. Genius, right? Here's my nod to that idea: a Triple Onion Cream Cheese–Stuffed Bagel Ball. I especially love serving these bagel balls in breakfast buffets (that was a lot of alliteration on accident!), because there's no hold up in the line from spreading on cream cheese. It's already right there, ready to roll (so punny!).

MAKES 6 BAGEL BALLS

1 cup (120 g) self-rising flour, plus more for work surface

1 cup (250 g) plain Greek yogurt

½ tsp onion powder

4 oz (115 g) cream cheese, softened

2 tbsp (6 g) minced scallions

Salt and pepper

1 egg, beaten

1 tbsp (5 g) dried onions

Preheat the oven to 425°F (220°C). Line a baking sheet with parchment paper and set it aside.

In a medium bowl, using a wooden spoon, combine the flour, yogurt and onion powder until a shaggy dough forms. Generously flour a work surface. Transfer the dough to the work surface and knead it a few times until a smooth dough forms. Divide the dough into six equal pieces; roll each piece into a ball and then flatten it slightly into a disk.

Switch tasks for just a moment. In a small bowl, combine the cream cheese and scallions and season with salt and pepper. Using a teaspoon, scoop one-sixth of the cream cheese mixture into a small ball. Place the cream cheese into the center of a dough round and bring the edges of the dough around the cream cheese to enclose. Turn the ball over so that it is seam side down and place it on the prepared baking sheet. Repeat the process with the remaining dough and cream cheese.

Brush the dough balls with the beaten egg and sprinkle with the dried onions. Bake for 18 to 20 minutes, or until they are golden brown. Let the balls cool for 5 minutes before eating. The cream cheese will be very hot at first, so use caution on your first bite! These are also wonderful at room temperature, so make them ahead whenever you'd like.

SUN-DRIED TOMATO PESTO CREAM CHEESE–STUFFED BAGEL BALLS

I had so much fun creating (and eating!) cream cheese–stuffed bagel balls, so I had to amp up the fun by making a few more flavors based on some of my favorite flavor combos. These bagels have a super flavorful center made from sun-dried tomato pesto and cream cheese. If you like cold pizza for breakfast, you'll want to wake up to one of these babies.

MAKES 6 BAGEL BALLS

1 cup (120 g) self-rising flour, plus more for work surface

1 cup (250 g) plain Greek yogurt

½ tsp Italian seasoning, plus more for sprinkling on the top

4 oz (115 g) cream cheese, softened

2 tbsp (30 g) prepared sun-dried tomato pesto

Salt and pepper

1 egg, beaten

Preheat the oven to 425°F (220°C). Line a baking sheet with parchment paper and set aside.

In a medium bowl, using a wooden spoon, combine the flour, yogurt and Italian seasoning until a shaggy dough forms. Generously flour a work surface. Transfer the dough to the work surface and knead a few times until a smooth dough forms.

Divide the dough into six equal pieces; roll each piece into a ball and flatten the balls slightly into a disk. In a small bowl, combine the cream cheese and pesto. Season with salt and pepper. Using a teaspoon, scoop one-sixth of the cream cheese mixture into a small ball. Place in the center of a dough disc and bring the edges of the dough around the cream cheese to enclose. Turn the ball over so that the seam side is down and place on the prepared baking sheet. Repeat the process with the remaining dough.

Brush the dough balls with the beaten egg. Sprinkle with the additional Italian seasoning and bake for 18 to 20 minutes, or until they are golden brown. Let the balls cool for 5 minutes before eating. The cream cheese will be very hot at first, so use caution.

CHEDDAR, ONION AND BLACK PEPPER VISITING LOAF

Here's a quick loaf that's perfect for sharing, a cousin to the blueberry-lemon loaf that appears in the Sweets and Treats section (page 135), except this loaf is a savory, cheesy one. It would be the perfect quick-to-make loaf to bring to a friend with a quart of homemade soup. You had better make two though, because your family's going to want some too! You can leave out the black pepper, or you can double it for an added bit of excitement.

SERVES 6

1 cup (250 g) plain Greek yogurt

1¼ cups (150 g) self-rising flour

1 egg

1 cup (125 g) extra-sharp cheddar cheese, coarsely shredded

2 tbsp (10 g) dried onion

1 tsp freshly ground black pepper

All-purpose flour, for work surface

Butter, for serving

Preheat the oven to 425°F (220°C). Line a baking sheet with parchment and set aside.

In a medium bowl, using a wooden spoon, combine the yogurt, self-rising flour and egg. The dough will be very sticky. Add the cheese, onions and pepper to the dough. Generously coat a work surface with all-purpose flour. Turn out the dough onto the work surface and knead a few times, just until somewhat smooth but still a bit sticky.

Shape the dough into a 7- to 8-inch (18- to 20-cm) diameter round. Dust the top of the loaf generously with all-purpose flour. Using a sharp knife, cut four slashes (one horizontal, one vertical and two diagonals in the shape of an X) across the top of the dough to form a snowflake-type shape, for decoration and for helping to release steam.

Transfer the loaf to the baking sheet. Bake for about 20 to 22 minutes on the middle rack of the oven, or until the dough is a deep golden brown and the cracks on the top are dry to the touch. Let the loaf cool for at least 10 minutes before slicing into wedges and serving with a generous spreading of butter.

PITA POCKETS WITH CUCUMBER RAITA

After storing a batch of two-ingredient dough in the refrigerator for 24 hours, I accidentally discovered that the dough makes a perfectly-puffed pita! I've had luck with storing the dough in the fridge for just a few hours, but the most reliable puffs come after the dough is thoroughly chilled, at least overnight. If the dough tears while you're rolling it out, gather it back up into a ball and start again, or you won't get a pocket. If you don't get a pocket, just pretend like you meant to make a delicious, non-pocketed flatbread. No one will be the wiser.

MAKES 4

1 cup (120 g) self-rising flour, plus more for work surface

1 cup (250 g) plain Greek yogurt

1 tbsp (6 g) nigella seeds, optional

CUCUMBER RAITA

1 cucumber

1 tbsp (15 ml) lemon juice

1 tbsp (15 ml) olive oil

½ cup (125 g) plain Greek yogurt

1 clove garlic, minced

Salt and pepper, to taste

Line a baking sheet with parchment paper and set aside.

In a medium bowl, combine the flour and 1 cup (250 g) yogurt using a wooden spoon until a shaggy dough forms. Generously flour a work surface. Turn out the dough onto the work surface and knead it about ten times, just until the dough can come together in a mostly smooth ball. Gather the dough into a ball and place in a plastic zip-top bag. Refrigerate overnight or for up to 72 hours.

When you're ready to bake, remove the dough from the fridge. Preheat the oven to 425°F (220°C). Using a sharp knife, divide the dough into four equal sections. On a generously floured work surface, press each dough section into a circular shape about 6 inches (15 cm) in diameter, being careful not to tear the dough. Sprinkle the tops of the pitas with the nigella seeds, if you are using them. Place the pitas on the baking sheet and bake for 12 to 14 minutes, or until they are golden brown and puffy.

To make the Cucumber Raita, peel and grate the cucumber into a medium dish. Dry the cucumber with a paper towel by squeezing off any additional moisture. Add the lemon juice, olive oil, ½ cup (125 g) of plain Greek yogurt and garlic to the cucumber. Season the mixture to taste with salt and pepper. Serve with the pockets.

ISRAELI SESAME RING BREAD
WITH SALT AND HERBS FOR DIPPING

In college, when I was on a study abroad in Jerusalem, my friends and I would walk into the city and buy round sesame bread, nicknamed Jerusalem bagels. The vendors hand you the warm bagels with a small paper package full of Middle Eastern herbs—zaatar and salt—for dipping into with the bread. If you can't find zaatar, a combination of finely chopped cilantro and mint makes a good substitute.

MAKES 3 BAGELS

1 cup (120 g) self-rising flour, plus more for work surface

1 cup (250 g) plain Greek yogurt

2 tsp (8 g) sugar, divided

1 egg, beaten

2 tbsp (20 g) sesame seeds

1 tbsp (15 g) sea salt, for serving

1 tbsp (2 g) zaatar, for serving, or substitute chopped fresh cilantro and mint

Preheat the oven to 425°F (220°C) and line a baking sheet with parchment paper.

In a medium bowl, combine the flour, yogurt and 1 teaspoon of sugar, using a wooden spoon, until a shaggy dough forms. Set the spoon aside and knead the dough a few times until it comes together in a smooth ball. Divide the dough into three equal-sized pieces.

Generously flour a work surface. Roll each piece of dough on the work surface to form a snake about 12 inches (30 cm) long. Join the ends together to make a circle, pinching the pieces to close. It should look like a skinny bagel. Transfer the bagels to the prepared baking sheet. If you want to make them look like the real Jerusalem bagels, stretch the bagels so the shape is more of an elongated oval than a circle.

Brush each bagel top and sides with the beaten egg and sprinkle with the sesame seeds and the remaining teaspoon of sugar. Bake for 18 to 20 minutes, or until they are golden brown. Let the rings cool for 10 minutes before serving, passing the sea salt and zaatar combined in small bowls for dipping.

RUSTIC OLIVE, FETA AND ROASTED RED PEPPER LOAF

Years ago, I went out to an Italian restaurant in Santiago, Chile. The waiter brought a round loaf before the meal began. Silly me, I thought it was fruitcake, since the loaf was studded with colorful objects and dusted with what I believed was powdered sugar. I was wrong, and delighted to be wrong, since I wasn't about to eat any fruitcake. The loaf was savory, studded not with candied fruits but with olives and peppers and dusted with a coating of flour. It was so good that our table of five ate three rustic loaves with our dinner that night. Who needs dinner when the bread is so good?

SERVES 6

1 cup (120 g) self-rising flour, plus more for work surface

1 cup (250 g) plain Greek yogurt

2 tbsp (30 ml) olive oil

½ cup (90 g) mixed olives—I like a combination of black and green oil–cured olives

½ cup (75 g) jarred red peppers, drained and chopped

½ tsp dried rosemary

3 oz (85 g) crumbled feta cheese

Additional olive oil and balsamic vinegar, for dipping, optional

Preheat the oven to 425°F (220°C), and line a baking sheet with parchment paper.

In a medium bowl, combine the flour and yogurt until it forms a shaggy dough. Stir in the olive oil, olives, peppers, rosemary and feta.

Generously flour a work surface. Remove the dough to the work surface and knead a few times, just until the dough comes together into a smooth ball. Transfer the dough to the baking sheet and press into a disk, around 7 inches (18 cm) in diameter. Dust the dough generously with flour. Bake for 22 to 25 minutes, or until the loaf is a deep golden brown. Serve with olive oil and balsamic vinegar for dipping, if you like.

RED ONION AND GRUYÈRE FOUGASSE

If you've never had *fougasse*, you should know that it is just the French cousin of Italian focaccia. My version of fougasse is extra flavorful with sautéed red onions, cubes of melted Gruyère and just a touch of rosemary. Fougasse is typically cut into a leaf or tree shape, making it easy to tear off a single serving, although one serving is never enough for me.

SERVES 4

1 tbsp (15 ml) olive oil

½ large red onion, chopped

1 cup (120 g) self-rising flour, plus more for work surface

1 cup (250 g) plain Greek yogurt

4 oz (115 g) Gruyère cheese, cut into ½-inch (1.3-cm) cubes

½ tsp dried rosemary, crumbled

Preheat the oven to 425°F (220°C), and line a baking sheet with parchment paper.

In a medium saucepan over medium heat, warm the olive oil. Add the onion and sauté until it just begins to soften, about 5 minutes. Remove it from the heat. In a medium bowl, stir together the flour and the yogurt. Gently stir in the onion, cheese and rosemary.

Generously flour a work surface. Pat the dough into an oval, around 12 x 7 inches (30 x 18 cm), but don't be too precise. Transfer the dough to the parchment-lined baking sheet. Starting at almost the top of the dough, make a vertical cut down the center, not cutting all the way through at the top or the bottom. Make three diagonal cuts on each side of the vertical cut, forming a leaf shape. Using your fingers, gently stretch the cuts open.

Bake for about 18 to 20 minutes, or until it's golden brown. Immediately after you remove the fougasse from the oven, use a knife to reopen the cuts you made before baking. Let the fougasse cool for at least 5 minutes.

MONTEREY JACK CHEESE, DILL AND SCALLION BISCUITS

I love biscuits with barbecue in the summertime and with pot roasts in the winter. Biscuits come together so quickly, but like all warm breads, they make a meal seem almost holiday-special. If you have any leftover biscuits, these make a spectacular sandwich with leftover shredded barbecue meat and a little coleslaw.

MAKES 6 BISCUITS

1½ cups (180 g) self-rising flour, plus more for work surface

1½ cups (375 g) plain Greek yogurt

3 tbsp (40 g) cold butter

½ cup (70 g) Monterey Jack cheese, shredded

¼ cup (13 g) sliced scallions

2 tbsp (30 ml) butter, melted

½ tsp garlic powder

1 tsp dried dill weed

Preheat the oven to 425°F (220°C), and line a baking sheet with parchment paper.

In a medium bowl, mix the flour and yogurt until just combined. Grate the cold butter, using the large holes from a box grater, directly into the bowl with the flour and yogurt. Gently stir together. Stir in the shredded cheese and scallions.

Dust a work surface generously with flour. Transfer the dough to the work surface and knead until smooth, about 30 seconds. Press the dough into a rectangle, about 9 x 6 inches (23 x 15 cm). Using a sharp knife, cut the dough into six equal-shaped square biscuits. Transfer the biscuits to the baking sheet, spacing about 2 inches (5 cm) apart.

In a small bowl, combine the melted butter, garlic powder and dill. Brush about half of the butter mixture over the tops of the biscuits. Bake for about 16 minutes, or until they are golden brown. Remove the biscuits from the oven and brush them with the remaining butter mixture. Cool for 5 minutes before eating.

CHEDDAR AND OLD BAY BUTTER-TOPPED DROP BISCUITS

These biscuits remind me of the popular starter at a well-known seafood chain. You know those little biscuits that always get devoured before the food arrives? Everyone loves them. The texture on these biscuits is rough and craggy, perfect for collecting the melted, Old Bay-enriched butter.

MAKES 10 BISCUITS

1 cup (120 g) self-rising flour

1 cup (250 g) plain Greek yogurt

2 tbsp (30 g) cold butter

½ cup (65 g) sharp cheddar cheese, grated

2 tbsp (30 ml) butter, melted

1 tsp Old Bay seasoning

½ tsp garlic powder

Preheat the oven to 425°F (220°C), and line a baking sheet with parchment paper.

In a medium bowl, combine the flour and yogurt until just combined. Grate the cold butter, using the large holes from a box grater, directly into the bowl with the flour and yogurt. Add the shredded cheese to the bowl. Gently stir together.

Using a spoon, form ten imperfect biscuits and plop them onto the prepared baking sheet. They should look irregular and craggy.

In a small bowl, combine the melted butter, Old Bay seasoning and garlic powder. Spoon a little of the melted butter over the biscuits, reserving about half of the butter.

Bake the biscuits for about 15 minutes, or until they are golden brown. Remove them from the oven. Spoon the remaining butter mixture over the tops of the biscuits. Let the biscuits cool for 5 minutes before eating.

POPPY SEED HAMBURGER BUNS

If I'm going to eat a juicy cheeseburger, then I want a very fresh, golden hamburger bun. These are so much easier and faster than making yeast-risen hamburger buns, and they're even more delicious. I love these buns with beef burgers, turkey burgers, black bean burgers or even just a grilled, marinated portobello mushroom cap. You might want to double or triple this recipe if you're expecting a crowd for a cookout. I never, ever buy hamburger buns anymore. If you're watching calories or saturated fat, the buns also work well without the addition of butter.

MAKES 6 BUNS

2½ cups (300 g) self-rising flour, divided

2 cups (500 g) plain Greek yogurt

2 tbsp (30 ml) butter, melted

2 eggs

2 tbsp (30 ml) milk

1 tbsp (9 g) poppy seeds

Preheat the oven to 425°F (220°C). Line a baking sheet with a piece of parchment paper.

In a medium bowl, using a wooden spoon, combine 2 cups (240 g) of flour, yogurt, butter and eggs. Stir until the mixture forms a sticky ball. Sprinkle ½ cup (60 g) of flour onto a work surface, maybe more if you need it. Turn out the dough onto the surface and knead for 1 minute, allowing the dough to absorb the additional flour from the work surface. If the dough is still too sticky, add a little more flour. The sticky dough makes for a tender bun, so don't go overboard with adding the flour.

Divide the dough into six equal pieces. Shape each piece into a circle and flatten slightly to form a bun shape. Place on the prepared sheet. Brush the rolls with milk and sprinkle with poppy seeds.

Bake the buns for 18 to 20 minutes, or until they are golden brown. Remove them from the oven and allow to cool for 20 minutes. Slice the buns horizontally and serve immediately, or cool them completely and store in an airtight container for up to 3 days at room temperature, or freeze, tightly wrapped, for up to 3 months.

GERMAN SEEDED RYE ROLLS

If you've ever wandered into a Dutch or German bakery, then you know the pleasure of fragrant, dark breads and rolls studded with nuts and seeds. Now you can stay home and experience that old-world charm from the comfort of your own kitchen. A note: you won't necessarily taste the molasses or the cocoa powder, but they both lend complexity and that characteristic dark color of German breads. I like these German Seeded Rye Rolls best with a slice or two of deli ham, maybe some mild cheese, a bold mustard and pickle, but they are also delicious with a spread of cold, salted butter.

MAKES 4 ROLLS

1 cup (115 g) Self-Rising Rye Wheat Flour Blend (see note), plus more for work surface

1 cup (250 g) plain Greek yogurt

1 tbsp (7 g) cocoa powder, not Dutch process

1 tbsp (15 ml) molasses

1 egg, beaten

1 tbsp (7 g) caraway seeds

Preheat the oven to 425°F (220°C), and line a baking sheet with parchment paper.

In a medium bowl, using a wooden spoon, combine the Self-Rising Rye Wheat Flour Blend, yogurt, cocoa powder and molasses until the mixture forms a shaggy dough. Generously sprinkle flour onto a work surface. Turn out the dough onto the floured work surface and knead the dough a few times, for about 1 minute, until it forms a slightly sticky ball of dough, working in additional flour as needed to create a workable dough.

Gather your dough into a large ball. Cut the ball into four somewhat-equal pieces. Form each piece into an oval, about 2 x 4 inches (5 x 10 cm). Don't be too fussy here. You want your rolls to look handmade and rustic. Place your rolls on the prepared baking sheet.

Brush each roll with the beaten egg and sprinkle with the caraway seeds. Now let's decorate the tops. Make two lengthwise slashes with a knife on the top of the roll to form a V shape; make an additional slash down the center of the V. Bake the rolls for 18 to 20 minutes, or until the rolls are dark brown on the tops. Remove the rolls from the oven and let them cool for at least 20 minutes before serving.

NOTE: To make the Self-Rising Rye Wheat Flour Blend, in a medium bowl, combine ½ cup (70 g) whole-wheat flour, ½ cup (50 g) rye flour, 2 teaspoons (8 g) baking powder, ¼ teaspoon baking soda and ¾ teaspoon salt.

IRISH DILLY-RYE LOAF

My mother used to make Irish dilly-rye loaves with potato soup on chilly winter afternoons. I still like this loaf best with silky potato soup, but it's also very good on its own with creamy Irish butter or a wedge of Irish cheddar or best of all with all three—soup, butter and cheese.

SERVES 6

1 cup (115 g) Rye Self-Rising Flour (see note)

1 tsp caraway seeds

1 tsp dill seeds

1 cup (250 g) plain Greek yogurt

All-purpose flour, for work surface

Preheat the oven to 425°F (220°C). Line a baking sheet with parchment paper.

In a medium bowl, using a wooden spoon, combine the Rye Self-Rising Flour, caraway seeds, dill seeds and yogurt, stirring until a shaggy dough forms.

Generously flour a work surface with all-purpose flour. Turn out the dough onto the work surface. Knead until smooth, about 1 minute. Shape the dough into a ball and flatten into about a 5-inch (13-cm) diameter disk.

Place the dough on the prepared baking sheet and cut a big, wide X on the top of the loaf. Bake for 20 to 22 minutes, or until the dough is golden brown and dry in the cracks of the X. Let the bread cool for at least 20 minutes before slicing and serving.

NOTE: To make the Rye Self-Rising Flour, in a medium bowl, combine ½ cup (50 g) of rye flour, ½ cup (65 g) of all-purpose flour, ¼ teaspoon of baking soda, 2 teaspoons (8 g) of baking powder and ¾ teaspoon of salt.

SOFT AND BUTTERY DINNER ROLLS

These rolls look dressed up, like a holiday dinner or Sunday dinner kind of roll, except that since they're made with a base of two-ingredient dough, they come together in a snap. The butter in the rolls will melt out a little during the baking process, but just rub the bottoms of the rolls in any melted butter after baking, and the butter will soak right back in. If you want the rolls to look their prettiest, refrigerate the dough for at least two hours before forming the rolls.

MAKES 8 ROLLS

1 cup (120 g) self-rising flour, plus more for work surface

1 cup (250 g) plain Greek yogurt

3 tbsp (45 ml) butter, melted

1 tbsp (15 g) butter, softened

Preheat the oven to 425°F (220°C), and line a baking sheet with parchment paper.

In a medium bowl, combine the flour, yogurt and melted butter until just combined.

Generously flour a work surface, transfer the dough to the floured surface. Knead a few times, just until the dough comes together in a smooth ball. Add more flour to the work surface. Press the dough into a circular shape, about 10 inches (25 cm) in diameter. Spread the softened butter onto the dough. Cut the dough into eight equal-sized wedges. Roll up each wedge, tucking the loose ends underneath. If the dough tears or gets a hole in any place, just gently pinch it back together.

Place the rolls on the prepared baking sheet and bake for about 16 minutes, or until they are golden brown. Some of the butter may melt out of the rolls, so when the rolls come out of the oven, you can rub the roll bottoms in any of the melted butter to help absorb it back in. Let them cool for 10 minutes before serving. Pile the rolls into a basket lined with a cloth napkin.

PESTO-PARMESAN TWISTS

I keep two big basil plants alive and thriving between early spring and late fall every year. I especially like to make these breadsticks for summer parties, since I've always got fresh, homemade pesto on hand made from those two big basil plants, but store-bought pesto works great here too. I like to serve these breadsticks on a platter with sliced garden heirloom tomatoes and a drizzle of balsamic vinegar.

SERVES 4

1 cup (250 g) plain Greek yogurt

1 cup (120 g) self-rising flour, plus more for work surface

1 tbsp (6 g) Italian seasoning, plus more for garnish

3 tbsp (45 g) prepared pesto

⅓ cup (60 g) finely shredded Parmesan cheese, plus more for garnish

Preheat the oven to 425°F (220°C). Line a baking sheet with parchment paper and set it aside.

In a medium bowl, using a wooden spoon, combine the yogurt, flour and Italian seasoning to form a shaggy ball of dough. Set your spoon aside and knead the dough with your hands for 1 minute to form a smooth dough ball.

Generously coat a work surface with flour. Press or roll your dough into a rectangle, about 13 x 8 inches (33 x 20 cm). Spread the pesto onto the dough and sprinkle with Parmesan cheese. Cut the dough lengthwise into four equal breadsticks. Gently transfer each breadstick, spacing evenly, onto the baking sheet. Grasp one breadstick at the center and twist twice to form two twists on half of the breadstick. Grasp the breadstick at the center and twist twice again on the opposite end. The dough will be tender, so if it tears or breaks, just pinch it back together. Repeat the twisting process for each of the remaining breadsticks. If you like, sprinkle the tops of the breadsticks with additional Parmesan cheese and Italian seasoning.

Bake the breadsticks for about 18 to 20 minutes, or until the tops are golden brown and cheese is melted and bubbly. Let the breadsticks cool for 10 minutes before serving.

SPICY PEPPER JACK JALAPEÑO ROLL-UPS

My kids like their food seriously spicy. If I don't make these roll-ups spicy enough, Sailor and West will douse them with extra hot sauce. If you like your food more mild than wild, just use a milder sauce (even salsa would work), and use jack cheese without the hot peppers. These will still be delicious, even if you walk on the mild side.

MAKES 8

1 cup (120 g) self-rising flour, plus more for work surface

1 cup (250 g) plain Greek yogurt

1 tsp chili powder

½ tsp garlic powder

2 tbsp (6 g) scallions, chopped

2 tbsp (8 g) cilantro leaves, chopped, plus more for garnish

2 tbsp (30 ml) hot sauce—I like green hot sauces here

¾ cup (100 g) pepper jack cheese, shredded, plus more if desired

Preheat the oven to 425°F (220°C). Line a baking sheet with parchment paper.

In a medium bowl, using a wooden spoon, mix together the flour and yogurt until the mixture forms a shaggy dough. Set the spoon aside and knead the dough by hand in the bowl for 1 minute, or until the dough forms a smooth ball.

Generously sprinkle flour onto a work surface, and turn out the dough onto it. Press or roll the dough into a rectangle that measures roughly 12 x 6 inches (30 x 15 cm), dusting with more flour as needed as you go. Sprinkle the chili powder, garlic powder, scallions and cilantro onto the dough. Drizzle the hot sauce onto the dough and sprinkle with the cheese. Roll up the dough, starting with the long edge, into a cylinder shape, just like you might do with cinnamon rolls. Pinch the edges shut. Cut the dough into eight equal pieces. If they tear a little, just pinch them back together. Place the rolls on the baking sheet and sprinkle the tops of the rolls with additional cheese, if you like things extra cheesy.

Bake the rolls for about 20 to 22 minutes, or until the tops are completely golden brown. Let the rolls cool for 10 minutes on the baking sheet before serving. Sprinkle the rolls with additional cilantro leaves, if you like, and arrange on a platter. Maybe leave some hot sauce nearby for people—like my kids—who want an extra dose of heat.

BUTTERY HONEY DIJON-GLAZED SOFT PRETZELS

One day after eating soft pretzels that I was plunking into sauce over and over again, I wondered why I didn't just put the sauce right on the pretzel. What followed was many attempts to get the balance of sweet and mustardy and buttery just right. Aha! A little more honey and butter than mustard is the trick here. I think you're going to love them.

MAKES 4 PRETZELS

1 cup (120 g) self-rising flour, plus more for work surface

1 cup (250 g) plain Greek yogurt

1 egg, beaten

1 tbsp (15 ml) butter, melted

1 tbsp (15 ml) honey

2 tsp (10 ml) Dijon mustard

1 tsp poppy or chia seeds

Preheat the oven to 425°F (220°C). Line a baking sheet with parchment paper and set aside.

In a medium bowl, combine the flour and yogurt with a wooden spoon, just until a shaggy dough forms. Set the spoon aside and knead the dough in the bowl until it forms a smooth ball, about 1 minute.

Dust a work surface generously with flour. Divide the dough into four equal pieces. Roll each dough piece into an 18-inch (46-cm) snake. If the dough is too sticky, roll it around in a light coating of flour. If the dough resists rolling, wet your hands very slightly and roll with moist hands. Shape each snake into a pretzel by grasping the two ends of the dough and crossing over into the center. Transfer shaped pretzels to the prepared baking sheet. Brush each pretzel with the beaten egg. Bake the pretzels for 15 to 18 minutes, or until deeply golden brown.

Meanwhile, in a small bowl, combine the butter, honey and mustard. When the pretzels come out of the oven, immediately brush them with the warm honey mixture on both sides. If any of the honey mixture remains, wait a few minutes and brush it on the pretzels again. After the last brushing of honey, lightly sprinkle with poppy seeds.

PRETZEL BITES
WITH SWEET AND TANGY CHEESE SAUCE

Say hello to these party pretzels, just one bite each, making it so easy to pop a few of them into your mouth. The cheese sauce itself is highly addictive and so easy to make. With the tiny pretzel size, you won't have to worry about anyone double dipping, but you might catch people sneaking a few bites of cheese sauce with a spoon when the pretzels are gone, which will happen pretty darn fast.

SERVES 6

PRETZELS

1 cup (120 g) self-rising flour, plus more for work surface

1 cup (250 g) plain Greek yogurt

⅓ cup (70 g) baking soda, for the boiling water

Pretzel salt or coarse sea salt

CHEESE SAUCE

8 oz (230 g) cheddar cheese, coarsely chopped or grated

5 tbsp (75 ml) apple juice or water

1–2 tsp (5–10 g) prepared horseradish (use the larger amount for more heat)

Preheat the oven to 425°F (220°C). Line a baking sheet with parchment paper; coat the parchment paper with cooking spray and set aside.

In a medium bowl, combine the flour and yogurt by stirring with a wooden spoon until the mixture forms a shaggy ball. Set the wooden spoon aside and knead the mixture in the bowl by hand for about ten turns, until the dough is relatively smooth. Gather the dough into a ball.

Generously flour a work surface and turn out the dough onto the surface. Divide the dough into four equal pieces. Roll each piece into a snake about 15 inches (38 cm) long. Cut each snake into 15 (1-inch [2.5-cm]) pieces, creating 60 total bites. Meanwhile, boil 6 cups (1.4 L) of water in a large pot. Slowly add the baking soda to the water. The water will bubble up vigorously, so be sure to add the baking soda carefully. Add about one-third of the pretzel bites to the water. Boil for 30 seconds. Remove the pretzel bites with a slotted spoon and place them on the prepared baking sheet, spacing evenly, so that the pretzels do not touch one another. Repeat the process until all the pretzel bites have been boiled.

Sprinkle the pretzel bites with the pretzel salt. Transfer to the oven and bake for about 12 to 15 minutes, or until they are well browned.

Prepare the cheese sauce by processing the cheese, apple juice and desired amount of horseradish in a food processor until smooth and creamy. Transfer to a small bowl. Serve the pretzel bites with the cheese sauce.

GIANT CREAM CHEESE AND JALAPEÑO-STUFFED PRETZEL FOR A CROWD

This is a bit of a stunt pretzel. It just looks fun to see a face-sized pretzel staring back at you, especially a pretzel that you know is stuffed with cream cheese and jalapeños. Be patient when you're rolling out the pretzel dough. If it resists rolling, wet your hands lightly with water and try again. If the dough is sticky, add more flour to your work surface. You might need to alternate between both techniques during the process. Get your camera ready, since everyone likes to take a picture of themselves peering through the holes of this pretzel. It's an Instagram-worthy moment.

SERVES 4

1 cup (120 g) self-rising flour, plus more for work surface

1 cup (250 g) plain Greek yogurt

4 oz (115 g) cream cheese, softened

1 large jalapeño, seeded, stemmed and finely chopped

1 egg, beaten

2 tsp (12 g) pretzel salt or coarse sea salt

Preheat the oven to 425°F (220°C). Line a baking sheet with parchment paper.

In a medium bowl, combine the flour and yogurt until they come together in a ball. Generously flour a work surface.

Transfer the dough to the work surface and begin to roll the dough into a 24-inch (60-cm) snake shape, adding more flour if the dough sticks, or wetting your hands if the dough is dry and resists rolling. Set the snake aside briefly. Flour the work surface again. Roll the cream cheese on the floured work surface to form a 22-inch (55-cm) snake. Press the dough to flatten the snake shape slightly. Place the cream cheese snake on top of the flattened dough snake. Sprinkle the chopped jalapeños evenly over the cream cheese. Press the dough around the cream cheese and jalapeños to encase.

Transfer the giant rope of dough to the prepared baking sheet and shape into a pretzel, by creating a U shape with the dough, twisting the ends, and then pressing the ends back into the pretzel. Brush the pretzel with the egg and sprinkle with the pretzel salt.

Bake for about 22 minutes, or until the pretzel is a deep golden brown. If any of the cream cheese escapes during the baking process, it will just make the pretzel look even more inviting. Let it cool for 10 minutes before ripping off sections to share.

BUTTERY PARMESAN AND GARLIC KNOTS

These adorable little twists are reminiscent of pizza parlor rolls. They're heady with garlic, rich with butter and perky with Parmesan. It takes a little patience to roll out the twists, but it's well worth it. If you have company over for casual snacks, like, say, for watching NBA play-offs, pop these in the oven to make everyone go crazy with the inviting scent of butter and garlic. You might want to double this batch. One per person is nowhere near enough.

MAKES 12 KNOTS

1 cup (120 g) self-rising flour, plus more for work surface

1 cup (250 g) plain Greek yogurt

½ tsp garlic powder

1 tbsp (15 g) butter

1 tbsp (15 ml) extra virgin olive oil

1 large clove garlic, minced

2 tbsp (25 g) Parmesan cheese, finely grated

1 tbsp (4 g) fresh parsley, minced

Preheat the oven to 425°F (220°C). Line a baking sheet with parchment paper and set aside.

In a large bowl, using a wooden spoon, combine the flour, yogurt and garlic powder, stirring until a sticky dough forms.

Generously flour a work surface. Turn out the dough onto the work surface and knead a few times until the mixture becomes a smooth ball. Divide the dough in half, then divide each half in half again. Divide each piece of dough into three equal sections, until you have twelve pieces of dough that are roughly equal in size. Roll each piece of dough into a snake shape, about 8 inches (20 cm) long. Tie each snake into a knot at the center and transfer to the prepared baking sheet. I like to tuck the ends of the knot under the roll on some and leave the ends out on others. It makes the rolls visually interesting to have a variety of shapes.

Meanwhile, place the butter and olive oil in a small microwaveable dish. Microwave for 30 seconds, or until the butter melts. Whisk in the garlic and return the mixture to the microwave. Microwave for another 30 seconds, or until the mixture sizzles and the garlic is fragrant. Lightly brush each knot with some of the butter mixture, reserving the majority of the mixture for when the knots come out of the oven. Bake for 15 to 18 minutes, or until the knots are golden brown. Immediately brush the knots with the remaining butter mixture. Sprinkle with Parmesan and parsley.

BACON, FIG AND GRUYÈRE VOLCANO ROLLS

Oh, the cheese in these rolls comes oozing out of the spirals, spilling out over the top, pooling attractively around the edges. It's a thing of beauty, all that melted cheese, and a joy forever. The flavors of bacon, sweet fig jam and that melted cheese I can't stop talking about make these volcano rolls absolutely unforgettable.

MAKES 6 ROLLS

1 cup (120 g) self-rising flour, plus more for work surface

1 cup (250 g) plain Greek yogurt

¼ cup (80 g) fig preserves

½ cup (60 g) bacon, fully cooked, crumbled

1¼ cup (170 g) Gruyère or Swiss cheese, shredded, divided

Preheat the oven to 425°F (220°C). Line a baking pan with parchment paper and set aside.

In a medium bowl, combine the flour and yogurt, stirring until the dough just comes together.

Generously flour a work surface and transfer the dough to the surface. Knead a couple of times, just until the dough develops into a smooth ball. Flour the work surface again. Roll or press the dough into a rectangle, about 12 x 9 inches (30 x 23 cm). If the dough sticks, just gather it back up, reflour your surface, and begin again. Spread the preserves onto the dough and sprinkle with the bacon and ¾ cup (100 g) of cheese. Starting at the long end, roll the dough up as if you were making cinnamon rolls.

Cut the dough into six equally-shaped spirals. Place each spiraled roll on the prepared baking sheet, using your fingers to press the rolls open and flatten a bit. Cover each roll with the remaining ½ cup (70 g) of shredded cheese. Bake for about 18 minutes, or until the cheese is melted and oozy and browned. Let the rolls cool for a couple of minutes before serving.

FLATBREADS, PIZZAS AND MAIN DISH BREADS

Two-ingredient dough is for mealtime too. Mix up a little dough and you've got the start of pizzas, breakfast flatbreads, samosas, empanadas, quiche or even potpie. You'll find lots of quick and easy mealtime inspirations right here.

CARAMELIZED ONION, ASIAGO AND ROSEMARY FOCACCIA

We have a hearty rosemary bush near our front walkway outside of our home. When it rains, you can smell the clean, herbal scent of rosemary all the way to the front door. Once I smell that rosemary scent, I'm going to want to make focaccia. This version is particularly delicious with caramelized onions and Asiago cheese. If you don't have Asiago on hand, Parmesan would also work well.

SERVES 8

CARAMELIZED ONIONS

1 tbsp (15 ml) olive oil

2 large onions, thinly sliced

2 tsp (30 g) brown sugar

1 tsp balsamic vinegar

FOCACCIA

1 cup (120 g) self-rising flour

1 cup (250 g) plain Greek yogurt

3 tbsp (45 ml) olive oil, divided

1 tsp dried rosemary or fresh needles, plus more fresh rosemary for garnish, if desired

¾ cup (95 g) Asiago cheese, shredded

Preheat the oven to 425°F (220°C).

For the caramelized onions, in a medium saucepan, warm 1 tablespoon (15 ml) of olive oil over medium heat. Add the onions and stir around to coat with oil. Reduce the heat to medium-low and allow the onions to cook until they are golden brown and wilted, about 20 minutes. Stir in the brown sugar and balsamic vinegar. Cook the onions for 3 minutes and set aside.

For the focaccia, in a medium bowl, combine the flour, yogurt, 1 tablespoon (15 ml) of olive oil and rosemary with a wooden spoon until shaggy dough forms. Set the spoon aside and knead the dough in the bowl with your hand for 1 minute, or until the dough forms a smooth ball. Drizzle 1 tablespoon (15 ml) of olive oil into a glass pie dish. Press the dough into the dish right on top of the drizzled olive oil. Sprinkle the cheese onto the dough. Scatter the onions on top of the cheese. Drizzle again with the remaining tablespoon (15 ml) of olive oil.

Bake the focaccia for 22 to 24 minutes, or until the onions brown and the dough is risen and somewhat firm to the touch. Let the focaccia cool for 5 minutes. Garnish with fresh rosemary, if you like. Slice into eight wedges.

SPINACH, FETA AND RED BELL PEPPER
BREAKFAST FLATBREADS

Breakfast flatbreads have been extremely popular—maybe even more popular than cookies—on my Instagram account, and that's saying a lot! Flatbreads are easy, visually pleasing, nutritious and ready in minutes. With that beautiful egg on top, these are perfect for breakfast, but they would work well for brunch, lunch, dinner or a midnight snack too. If you want yours to be a little heartier, add some sliced, fully cooked sausage.

SERVES 4

1 cup (120 g) self-rising flour, plus more for work surface

1 cup (250 g) plain Greek yogurt

½ cup (15 g) baby spinach leaves

¼ cup (40 g) roasted red peppers

8 black olives, halved

8 cherry tomatoes, halved

4 eggs

Salt and pepper

4 oz (115 g) feta cheese, crumbled

Preheat the oven to 425°F (220°C). Line a baking sheet with parchment paper.

In a medium bowl, using a wooden spoon, combine the flour and yogurt just until a shaggy dough forms. Set the spoon aside and knead the mixture in the bowl until the mixture develops into a smooth ball, about 1 minute.

Dust a work surface generously with flour. Divide the dough into four equal pieces. Roll or press each dough section into an elongated oval, about 7 x 4 inches (18 x 10 cm). Place each oval onto the parchment-lined baking sheet.

Bake the naked pizzas for 3 minutes, or until just starting to set. Take them out of the oven and top each pizza with spinach, bell peppers, olives and tomatoes, dividing evenly. Using your fingers, make a small indentation in the middle of each flatbread. Move the vegetables out of the middle of the pizza to form a little nest. Crack an egg into the center of each nest, then sprinkle salt and pepper on each egg. Sprinkle the crumbled feta cheese onto the flatbreads, dividing evenly. Bake for 9 to 11 minutes, or until the egg is set to your liking, using the lesser time for a more liquid yolk.

MAPLE BACON, JALAPEÑO AND GRUYÈRE GOOD MORNING FLATBREADS

I make a lot of breakfast pizzas, and they never fail to please and impress. This one might be the crowd favorite, with that sweet maple bacon paired with spicy jalapeños. When we have visitors to our home in the red rock desert, this always seems like a perfect Southwest-themed breakfast. They make a complete brunch served with lots of fresh fruit with a squeeze of lime and a drizzle of honey.

SERVES 4

1 cup (120 g) self-rising flour, plus more for work surface

1 cup (250 g) plain Greek yogurt

½ cup (70 g) Gruyère, shredded

4 slices bacon, cooked and crumbled

1 jalapeño, thinly sliced into rings

4 eggs

Salt and pepper

1 tbsp (15 ml) pure maple syrup

2 tbsp (6 g) scallions, chopped

Preheat the oven to 425°F (220°C). Line a baking sheet with parchment paper and set aside.

In a medium bowl, using a wooden spoon, combine the flour and yogurt just until a shaggy dough forms. Set the spoon aside and knead the mixture in the bowl with your hand until you have a smooth ball, about 1 minute.

Dust a work surface generously with flour. Divide the dough into four equal pieces. Roll or press each dough section into an elongated oval, about 7 x 4 inches (18 x 10 cm). Place each oval onto the prepared baking sheet. Bake the naked pizzas for 3 minutes. Remove the pizzas from the oven and top each pizza with Gruyère, bacon and jalapeño, dividing evenly. Using your fingers, make a small indentation in the middle of each flatbread. Crack an egg into the center of each flatbread. Sprinkle salt and pepper on each egg.

Bake for 9 to 11 minutes, or until the egg is set to your liking, using the lesser time for a more liquid yolk. Drizzle each flatbread with maple syrup and sprinkle with a few scallions.

SUPER-FOOD CRISPY KALE, AVOCADO AND FRIZZLED EGG FLATBREADS

Some weeks I start Monday morning with the idea that I'm going to make it a perfect exercise and eating day. That usually only lasts till after lunch, and then my sweet tooth gets the better of me. I wanted to make an undeniably healthy morning-ish flatbread as sort of a weekend detox food. I was delighted to find that the kale would become as crispy as kale chips in the same amount of time that it takes to bake an egg, all perched atop the two-ingredient dough. You can make this with white flour, but I like wheat flour for this virtuous, yet delicious meal.

SERVES 4

1 cup (135 g) Whole-Wheat Self-Rising Flour (see note), plus more for work surface

1 cup (250 g) plain Greek yogurt

1 cup (70 g) curly kale, torn into large pieces

12 cherry tomatoes, halved

¼ cup (35 g) red onion, thinly sliced

4 eggs

4 tsp (60 ml) olive oil

Salt and pepper

1 avocado, peeled and sliced

1 lime, quartered

Sriracha powder, for serving

Preheat the oven to 425°F (220°C). Line a baking sheet with parchment paper.

In a large bowl, combine the Whole-Wheat Self-Rising Flour and the yogurt, stirring until the mixture develops into a sticky ball.

Generously flour a work surface and turn out the dough onto the surface. Knead a few times until the dough is no longer sticky, sprinkling in more flour as needed. Divide the dough into four equal pieces.

Roll or press the dough into oval shapes, about 7 inches (18 cm) long. Don't be fussy here, since any shape will work. Bake the flatbreads for 4 minutes. Remove them from the oven and place the kale leaves around the inner edges of each flatbread, leaving a little space in the middle for the egg. Cover the kale with the cherry tomatoes and red onion, dividing evenly. Carefully crack an egg into the center of each flatbread. Drizzle the olive oil over the vegetables and egg whites, dividing evenly among each flatbread. Season with salt and pepper.

Bake the flatbreads for 8 to 9 minutes, or until the eggs are set to your liking. Remove them from the oven. Add the avocado slices and lime wedges—for squeezing juice just before serving—to each flatbread and sprinkle with sriracha powder. Serve immediately.

NOTE: To make the Whole-Wheat Self-Rising Flour, combine 1 cup (135 g) of whole-wheat flour, 2 teaspoons (8 g) of baking powder, ¼ teaspoon of baking soda and ¾ teaspoon of salt.

SPICY ITALIAN SAUSAGE AND MOZZARELLA CALZONES

When my teenage son West is in the middle of swim season, I like to have a batch of these calzones on hand, a batch in the fridge and a batch in the freezer. West can dash through the door and essentially have a grab-and-go meal. I like to make plenty, since teenage boys, like hungry wolves, usually travel in packs. I make sure there's enough for West and all his friends.

SERVES 4

1 cup (120 g) self-rising flour, plus more for work surface

1 cup (250 g) plain Greek yogurt

3 tbsp (35 g) cornmeal, divided

1 cup (115 g) mozzarella cheese, shredded

2 Italian sausage links, cooked and sliced into circles

¼ cup (60 ml) marinara sauce, plus more for serving

1 egg, beaten

1 tbsp (15 ml) olive oil

1 tsp fennel seeds or Italian seasoning

Preheat the oven to 425°F (220°C). Line a baking sheet with parchment paper and set aside.

In a medium bowl, combine the flour, yogurt and 1 tablespoon (11 g) of cornmeal, stirring with a wooden spoon until the mixture forms a shaggy dough. Set the spoon aside and knead the dough for about 1 minute, or until a smooth ball forms.

Generously dust a work surface with flour and place the dough on the surface. Divide the dough into four equal sections. Roll or press each dough section into a circle, about 7 to 8 inches (18 to 20 cm) in diameter. Don't be too fussy, since with all Italian foods, rustic is best! Fill one side of each circle with ¼ cup (30 g) of mozzarella, some of the sausage and about a tablespoon (15 ml) of the marinara. Brush the outer ½-inch (1.3-cm) edge of the calzones with egg. Fold up the dough into a calzone shape, forming a half circle. Using a fork, press the edges of the calzones shut.

Place the calzones on the prepared baking sheet. Brush the outsides of the dough with the olive oil and sprinkle with the remaining 2 tablespoons (24 g) of cornmeal and the fennel seeds.

Bake for 18 to 20 minutes, or until the calzones are golden brown. Remove them from the oven and let the calzones cool for 5 minutes. Serve with additional marinara for dipping.

DENVER HAM AND CHEDDAR BREAKFAST POCKETS

I love to make Denver omelets after Easter when I'm sure to have loads of leftover ham. This fun little twist on a traditional Denver omelet makes it easy for one-and-done breakfasts in the morning. All the expected elements are there—ham, cheese, bell peppers, egg—but they're all enrobed in a handy, healthful pastry pocket.

SERVES 4

FILLING

1 tbsp (15 g) butter

½ cup (75 g) fully cooked ham, chopped

½ cup (60 g) bell peppers, chopped, preferably red and green

2 tbsp (6 g) scallions, chopped

5 eggs, beaten, divided

½ cup (65 g) cheddar cheese, shredded, plus more for outsides of calzones, if desired

POCKETS

1 cup (120 g) self-rising flour, plus more for work surface

1 cup (250 g) plain Greek yogurt

Preheat the oven to 425°F (220°C). Line a baking sheet with parchment paper and set aside.

In a medium saucepan, melt the butter over medium heat. Add the ham, bell pepper and scallions, and cook for 2 minutes, or until the bell pepper begins to soften. Set aside 1 tablespoon (15 ml) of the beaten eggs to use for an egg wash. Pour the remaining beaten eggs over the ham mixture. Scramble the eggs slightly underdone, or to your liking. Remove the eggs from the heat and stir in the cheddar cheese. Set the egg mixture aside.

In a medium bowl, combine the flour and yogurt, stirring with a wooden spoon until the mixture forms a shaggy dough. Set the spoon aside and use your hand to knead the dough in the bowl for about 1 minute, or until a smooth ball forms.

Generously dust a work surface with flour and place the dough on the surface. Divide the dough into four equal sections. Roll or press each dough section into a circle, about 7 to 8 inches (18 to 20 cm) in diameter. Fill one side of each circle with the egg mixture, dividing equally. Brush the outer ½-inch (1.3-cm) edge of each pocket with the reserved 1 tablespoon (15 ml) of the beaten egg. Fold up the dough into a calzone shape, forming a half circle. Using a fork, press the edges of the pocket shut.

Place the pockets on the prepared baking sheet. Sprinkle the tops with a little additional cheddar cheese, if you like. Bake for 18 to 20 minutes, or until the pockets are golden brown. Remove them from the oven and allow to cool for 5 minutes before serving.

BLACK BEAN AND PEPPER JACK BAKED HUEVOS RANCHEROS

After a recent trip through Central America with a several family members, I came home craving the healthy egg-bean-salsa-fresh tortilla breakfasts that we were served each morning on the patios of our hotels. The fresh two-ingredient dough makes an easy and fast stand-in for a fresh tortilla, especially since this version is enhanced with a little cornmeal.

SERVES 4

1 cup (120 g) self-rising flour, plus more for work surface

1 cup (250 g) plain Greek yogurt

2 tbsp (25 g) cornmeal

1 cup (135 g) pepper jack cheese, shredded

½ cup (65 g) canned black beans, rinsed and drained

Jalapeño slices, optional

4 eggs

Salt and pepper

Hot sauce

Avocado slices, for garnish

Cilantro leaves, for garnish, optional

Preheat the oven to 425°F (220°C). Line a baking sheet with parchment paper and set aside.

In a medium bowl, combine the flour, yogurt and cornmeal with a wooden spoon, just until a shaggy dough forms. Set the spoon aside and knead the mixture in the bowl until you've got a smooth ball, about 1 minute.

Dust a work surface generously with flour. Divide the dough into four equal pieces. Roll or press each dough section into an elongated oval, about 7 x 4 inches (18 x 10 cm). Place each oval onto the baking sheet. Bake the dough for 3 minutes. Top each dough oval with shredded pepper jack cheese, dividing evenly. Sprinkle the cheese with black beans, dividing evenly. Top with jalapeño slices, if using.

Using your fingers, push the cheese and beans out of the center of the flatbread to make a little nest for the egg. Crack an egg into the center of each dough oval. Sprinkle the eggs with salt and pepper. Bake for 9 to 11 minutes, or until the egg is set to your liking, using the lesser time for a more liquid yolk. Drizzle each flatbread with hot sauce and top with additional jalapeños, avocado and cilantro leaves, if desired.

CALIFORNIA PIZZA
WITH FRESH GREENS, OLIVES AND AVOCADO

I crave fresh greens every day, so most days—if not every day—I'll try to work in a salad at some point. Salad isn't a hard sell for me, however it is with my family, but not if it's on a pizza. This is the kind of pizza that won't weigh you down but will instead make you feel light and healthy when you've finished eating—grown-ups and kids alike! You'll notice there's no sauce on this pizza, and you could definitely add some if you like, but I like the clean flavor of the dressed greens with the cheesy dough. This combo of fresh greens, pizza, olives and avocado pays homage to the state I grew up in—California.

SERVES 4

1 cup (120 g) self-rising flour, plus more for work surface

1 cup (250 g) plain Greek yogurt

1½ cups (175 g) mozzarella cheese, shredded

2 cups (150 g) spring lettuce mix, preferably with red and green leaves

½ cup (75 g) grape tomatoes

¼ cup (35 g) red onion slices

1 tbsp (15 ml) balsamic vinegar

1 tbsp (15 ml) olive oil

Salt and pepper

¼ cup (50 g) California black olives, halved

1 avocado, cubed

½ cup (65 g) ricotta cheese

Preheat the oven to 425°F (220°C). Line a baking sheet with parchment paper and set it aside.

In a medium bowl, using a wooden spoon, combine the flour and yogurt until a shaggy dough forms.

Generously flour a work surface. Turn out the dough onto the work surface and knead a couple of times, just until a smooth dough forms, about 1 minute. Shape into a large ball of dough. Roll or press the dough into a 12 x 7-inch (30 x 18-cm) rectangle. Transfer the dough to the prepared baking sheet. Alternatively, you could work with the dough by pressing it straight into the baking sheet instead of on the work surface.

Sprinkle the dough with the mozzarella and bake it for about 12 to 14 minutes, or until the cheese is browned and the dough is puffed. Meanwhile, in a medium bowl, toss the lettuce mix with the tomatoes, red onion, vinegar and olive oil. Season the lettuce mixture generously with salt and pepper. When the pizza comes out of the oven, let it cool for 5 minutes, then top the pizza with the salad mixture. Scatter the olives and avocado over the top. Spoon a few dollops of the ricotta onto the pizza in random places. Cut the pizza into four large sections and serve immediately.

GRANDMA'S LONG ISLAND TOMATO AND HERB PIZZA

If you haven't tried a "Grandma"-style pizza from Long Island, New York, here is your big chance. The dough is on the thinner side, crispy with olive oil and topped not with sauce but with a cheesy coating of mozzarella and Parmesan, then covered with olive oil, garlic and herb-coated tomatoes, and finally a sprinkling of basil. Yes, it's as good, or better, than it sounds. With the two-ingredient dough, you could be eating this pizza faster than you could call out for delivery, and probably faster than you could get to Long Island.

SERVES 6

1½ cups (180 g) self-rising flour

1½ cups (375 g) plain Greek yogurt

3 tbsp (45 ml) olive oil, divided

2 (14-oz [400-g]) cans diced tomatoes, well drained

3 cloves garlic, minced

1 tsp dried basil

1 tsp dried oregano

1 tsp sugar

Salt and pepper

2½ cups (290 g) mozzarella cheese, shredded

½ cup (95 g) Parmesan cheese, shredded

2 tbsp (6 g) fresh basil, thinly sliced

Preheat the oven to 425°F (220°C).

In a medium bowl, combine the flour and yogurt to form a shaggy dough. Coat a standard baking sheet with 1 tablespoon (15 ml) of olive oil, spreading with your fingers to coat.

Press the dough into the baking sheet until it reaches to all the corners. You may want to coat the top of the dough with additional flour to make the stretching job a little easier and less sticky. Set the dough aside.

In a medium bowl, combine the remaining 2 tablespoons (30 ml) of olive oil with the tomatoes, garlic, basil, oregano and sugar. Season to taste with salt and pepper.

Sprinkle the dough with the mozzarella and Parmesan cheese. Spread the tomato mixture over the top of the cheese. Bake the pizza for about 18 minutes, or until the cheese is golden brown. Remove the pizza from the oven and top with the basil. Let it cool for a few moments and cut into squares.

FOUR SEASONS SHEET PAN PIZZA— PIZZA QUATTRO STAGIONI

This pizza is a bit of a showstopper, maybe a bit of a show off too. It's just so pretty to see a sheet pan full of four different pizza choices. If you're like me, you'll want a square of all four choices. If you've got picky eaters in your group, you could top one quadrant of the pizza with just plain cheese.

SERVES 6

Olive oil cooking spray

2 tbsp (25 g) cornmeal

1½ cups (180 g) self-rising flour, plus more for working with the dough

1½ cups (375 g) plain Greek yogurt

1 (14-oz [400-g]) can petite diced tomatoes, drained

3 tbsp (75 g) tomato paste

3 tbsp (45 ml) olive oil, divided

1 tsp garlic powder

½ tsp crushed red pepper flakes, optional

1 tsp dried basil

½ tsp dried oregano

Pinch of sugar

Salt and pepper

3 cups (345 g) mozzarella cheese, shredded

4 oz (115 g) cremini or button mushrooms, thinly sliced

3 oz (90 g) prosciutto, thinly sliced

1 cup (170 g) marinated artichoke hearts, drained and thinly sliced

3 large Roma tomatoes, thinly sliced

10–12 small basil leaves

Preheat the oven to 425°F (220°C). Coat a sheet pan with cooking spray and the cornmeal.

For the dough, in a medium bowl, combine the flour and yogurt until a shaggy dough forms. Knead the dough in the bowl for a few turns, just until the dough forms a smooth ball. Turn out the dough onto the prepared baking sheet. Press the dough into the pan, sprinkling the top of the dough with a bit of flour as needed to prevent sticking, until the dough reaches the edges of the pan.

For the sauce, in a medium bowl, combine the diced tomatoes, tomato paste, 1 tablespoon (15 ml) olive oil, garlic powder, red pepper flakes, basil, oregano and sugar. Season to taste with salt and pepper. Spread the pizza with 1 cup (240 ml) of the sauce, leaving a 1-inch (2.5-cm) border all around. Spread the mozzarella cheese on the pizza.

For the assembly, in a small bowl toss the mushrooms with 1 tablespoon (15 ml) olive oil. Place the mushrooms on one-fourth of the pizza, creating a square area for each of the seasons. Place the prosciutto on one-fourth of the pizza, the artichokes on another one-fourth of the pizza and finally the tomatoes and basil on the remaining quadrant, tucking the basil underneath the sliced tomatoes. Drizzle the tomatoes and basil with the remaining 1 tablespoon (15 ml) of olive oil.

Bake the pizza for about 22 minutes, or until the cheese is melted and beginning to brown. Let the pizza cool for about 5 minutes before serving.

DEEP-DISH CHICAGO-STYLE PIZZA

When we visit Chicago, we always hunt down a new-to-us deep dish pizzeria. We have family opinions now that run strong about which Chicago deep-dish pizza is the best. The two-ingredient dough works so perfectly here, since deep-dish pizza has a more biscuit-like dough than traditional thinner pizzas. You can top this with whatever you like, but my family likes to keep it simple and classic with a thick layer of cheese and lotsa pepperoni! There's a hefty layer of mozzarella cheese in the middle, but if you want to use less, the recipe will still work well.

SERVES 4

PIZZA

1 tbsp (15 ml) olive oil

⅔ cup (80 g) self-rising flour, plus more for working with the dough

⅔ cup (170 g) plain Greek yogurt

3 cups (345 g) mozzarella cheese, shredded

4 oz (120 g) pepperoni, sliced

½ cup (35 g) button mushrooms, thinly sliced

½ cup (70 g) red onion, thinly sliced

½ cup (60 g) green bell pepper, sliced into thin rings

½ cup (95 g) Parmesan cheese, shredded

SAUCE

1 cup (165 g) canned petite diced tomatoes, drained

½ tsp garlic powder

1 tsp basil

1 tbsp (15 ml) olive oil

Pinch of sugar

Preheat the oven to 425°F (220°C). Grease an 8- or 9-inch (20- or 23-cm) cake pan with 1 tablespoon (15 ml) of olive oil.

For the pizza, in a medium bowl, combine the flour and yogurt and stir for 1 minute, until thoroughly combined. Transfer the dough to the prepared cake pan.

Sprinkle a little flour on top of the dough and press into the pan so that the dough reaches the edges. Bake for 8 minutes, just until the dough is puffed and beginning to set. Remove the dough from the oven and top with the mozzarella cheese, half of the pepperoni, mushrooms, onion, bell pepper and the remaining pepperoni.

For the sauce, in a medium bowl, combine the drained tomatoes, garlic powder, basil, olive oil and sugar. Spread the sauce over the pepperoni. Top with the Parmesan. Bake the pizza for 13 minutes, or until the cheese is melted and bubbly. Let it cool for 5 minutes.

GOLDEN POTATO AND ROSEMARY PIZZA

In Italy, potato pizzas are baked in big rectangle sheets. You can buy it by the slab at many of the little corner shops. It might seem a little crazy to have potatoes on pizza dough—carb on carb here—but it's actually delicious. The little touch of fragrant rosemary is a beautiful complement to the creamy potatoes and rich olive oil.

SERVES 4

1 cup (120 g) self-rising flour

1 cup (250 g) plain Greek yogurt

4 tbsp (60 ml) olive oil, divided

3 Yukon gold potatoes, scrubbed, not peeled, and very thinly sliced into circles

¾ tsp salt

Freshly ground black pepper

1 tsp fresh rosemary leaves

Preheat the oven to 425°F (220°C). Line a baking sheet with parchment paper.

In a large bowl, combine the flour, yogurt and 1 tablespoon (15 ml) of the olive oil. Stir until just combined.

Press the dough onto the parchment paper, stretching the dough as thin as you can get it. It should almost come to the edges of a standard baking sheet.

In a medium bowl, combine remaining 3 tablespoons (45 ml) of olive oil, potato slices, salt and pepper. Arrange the potatoes on the pizza dough in a single layer, coming all the way to the edge. Sprinkle the rosemary over the potatoes.

Bake for about 30 minutes, or until the potatoes are browned at the edges and in a few spots. If you want your potatoes to be crispier and more browned, turn on the broiler for a few minutes, but watch closely!

30-MINUTE START-TO-FINISH PIZZA MARGHERITA

This is my true-love pizza. If it's on the menu, it will always be my first choice. I love it, especially when you have the freshest and best possible summer tomatoes and garden basil. Don't try to make this with pre-shredded mozzarella; it has to be fresh, water-packed mozzarella, cut in generous slices for melting into puddles on the pizza in order to be really wonderful. Work at a good clip, and you'll have summery pizza coming out of the oven within 30 minutes. If you want to make this like the *Napolitano* pizzas in Rome, just add a few chopped anchovies.

SERVES 6

2 tbsp (25 g) cornmeal

1 cup (120 g) self-rising flour, plus more for work surface

1 cup (250 g) plain Greek yogurt

3 tbsp (45 ml) best quality olive oil, divided

2 ripe plum tomatoes, cut into thin rounds, plus cherry or grape tomatoes

Sea salt and black pepper

1 (8-oz [230 g]) ball fresh mozzarella, cut into 16 pieces

10–12 small basil leaves

Preheat the oven to 450°F (220°C). Line a baking sheet, preferably unrimmed, with parchment paper and sprinkle with cornmeal.

In a large bowl, combine the flour and yogurt until a shaggy dough forms.

Generously flour a work surface. Turn out the dough onto the work surface and knead a few times, just until the dough comes together into a smooth ball. Transfer the dough to the prepared baking sheet. Press the dough into a circle about 12 inches (30 cm) in diameter, maybe building up a little rim for the outer edge of the crust, if you like. Brush the dough with 2 tablespoons (30 ml) of the olive oil. Place the tomatoes on the dough, spreading out evenly. Sprinkle the tomatoes with a little sea salt and pepper.

Place the pieces of mozzarella on top of and around the tomatoes, spreading out evenly. Top with the basil leaves and drizzle with the remaining tablespoon (15 ml) of olive oil. Bake the pizza for about 12 to 14 minutes, or until the edges are nicely browned and the mozzarella is melted. Let it cool for 10 minutes before cutting into six slices for serving.

OLIVE OIL, TOMATO AND HERB PIZZA AL CAPRICCIO

I was in the middle of writing this cookbook when we took a trip as a family to Italy. I ate pizza every day on our trip. Wouldn't you? One of my favorites was a plain, cheese-less thin pizza that you can buy in a slab at a corner store. The slab is heated in a blazing oven, then folded in half, like a sandwich, and placed in a waxed paper bag for eating and walking along the streets of Rome. The only thing that could make this pizza a little better would be a double-scoop of gelato afterward.

SERVES 4

1 cup (120 g) self-rising flour, plus more for work surface

1 cup (250 g) plain Greek yogurt

3 tbsp (45 ml) olive oil, divided, plus more for drizzling

¾ cup (185 g) crushed tomatoes, the best quality you can find (I like San Marzano)

Pinch of crushed red pepper flakes

Salt and pepper

2 tbsp (8 g) chopped fresh herbs for serving, such as basil, oregano, rosemary and parsley

Preheat the oven to 425°F (220°C). Line a baking sheet with parchment paper.

In a large bowl, combine the flour, yogurt, and 1 tablespoon (15 ml) of olive oil, stirring until just combined.

Generously flour a work surface. Place the dough on the work surface and knead a few times, just until a smooth ball is formed. Place the dough on the prepared parchment sheet. Press the dough into a flat, thin rectangle that almost reaches the edges.

In a small bowl, combine the tomatoes, crushed red pepper flakes, remaining 2 tablespoons (30 ml) of olive oil and salt and pepper to taste. Spread the tomato mixture all the way to the edge of the dough. Bake for 20 minutes, or until the tomato mixture is starting to dry out and the edges of the crust are browned. Drizzle the pizza with olive oil and sprinkle with the herbs. You can cut slabs and fold them in half to serve, or you can serve this pizza by the square slice.

SOUTHERN FRENCH OLIVE AND CAPER PISSALADIÈRE

Classic Provençal pissaladière should have strips of anchovy arranged decoratively over the top, but I fear that anchovy in America might go unappreciated, especially visible anchovy. Inspired by a recipe I saw online, I substitute the anchovy strips with crowd-friendly prosciutto. If you're an anchovy fan, just make it the right way and enjoy it like a Frenchman! If you want to sneakily introduce your friends to anchovy, you can add a tablespoon (15 g) of anchovy paste to the onions while they cook. You'll get all the flavor without any of the visual.

SERVES 6

2 tbsp (30 ml) olive oil

3 large yellow onions, thinly sliced

2 cloves garlic, minced

3 sprigs fresh thyme, leaves removed and woody stem discarded, or ¼ tsp dried thyme

2 cups (240 g) self-rising flour, plus more for work surface

2 cups (500 g) plain Greek yogurt

2 tbsp (30 ml) butter, melted

8 oz (240 g) prosciutto, rolled up and then cut into long, thin ribbons

Heat the oil in a large skillet over medium heat. Add the onions and cook, stirring often, until the onions are wilted, about 10 minutes. Add the garlic and thyme. Reduce the heat to low and continue cooking until the onions are golden and completely soft, about 10 minutes longer. Set aside to cool for 10 minutes.

Preheat the oven to 425°F (220°C). Line a baking sheet with parchment paper.

In a large bowl combine the flour, yogurt and melted butter. Generously flour a work surface. Turn out the dough onto the work surface and knead a few times until the dough is smooth.

Press the dough onto the parchment paper, spreading to the edge. Build up the dough around the edges to form a rim. Top the dough, except for the rim, with the onions, spreading evenly. Arrange the prosciutto into a diagonal pattern, creating three diagonal rows going both directions. Bake the pissaladière for 12 to 15 minutes, or until the dough is golden brown on the edges.

CLASSIC SAUSAGE AND PEPPERONI STROMBOLI

My freshman college roommate was a native Philadelphia girl. Late at night, when the lights were out and we were talking way later than is sensible for anyone, she would reminisce about all her favorite foods from back home. One night, she described Stromboli in great detail—a sort of rolled-up hot Italian sandwich filled with meats, sauce, vegetables and cheese. I decided then and there that I would visit her in Philadelphia for Stromboli—and a little American history—which I did that summer and many times since then.

SERVES 6

1 lb (455 g) bulk Italian sausage, ground, spicy or sweet

1 red bell pepper, sliced into strips

6 oz (170 g) button mushrooms, sliced

1¼ cups (150 g) self-rising flour, plus more for work surface

1¼ cups (315 g) plain Greek yogurt

2 cups (230 g) mozzarella cheese, shredded

¾ cup (180 ml) tomato sauce

1 tbsp (15 ml) olive oil

2 tsp (4 g) Italian seasoning, plus more for the top

4 oz (120 g) pepperoni

1 egg, beaten

In a large skillet over medium-high heat, begin to cook the sausage, breaking it up with the back of a spoon, until almost browned, but still pink in places, about 5 minutes. Add the bell pepper and mushrooms and cook until the vegetables are softened, about 7 minutes. Let the mixture cool slightly and drain away any excess fat.

Preheat the oven to 425°F (220°C) and line a standard baking sheet with parchment paper.

In a medium bowl, combine the flour and yogurt with a wooden spoon, stirring until a sticky dough forms. Generously flour a work surface. Turn out the dough onto the work surface and knead, adding a dusting of flour from time to time, until the dough is no longer sticky. Roll or press the dough into a rectangle about 15 x 10 inches (38 x 25 cm). Arrange the shredded cheese in a long line near the long edge of the dough, leaving a 4-inch (10-cm) margin. Drizzle with tomato sauce and olive oil, and sprinkle with Italian seasoning. Cover the cheese with the sausage mixture. Arrange the pepperoni evenly over the sausage, overlapping as necessary.

Roll up the dough, cinnamon roll style, until you have a tight cylinder, and pinch the edges shut. Transfer the dough to the prepared baking sheet. Brush the dough with the egg and sprinkle with additional Italian seasoning, if desired. Cut a few slits along the top of the dough to allow steam to escape. Bake the Stromboli for 14 to 18 minutes, or until it's golden brown. Let the Stromboli cool for about 10 minutes before slicing into segments and serving.

PHILADELPHIA CHEESESTEAK STROMBOLI

This hearty dish pays homage to the two great Philadelphia food favorites: cheesesteak and Stromboli. The debate rages on over what is the proper cheese for a Philly cheesesteak, but I prefer provolone here because it melts beautifully and adds a hint of creamy sweetness. You could swap out the provolone for any cheese you like. One more note: this Stromboli is a Superbowl tradition at my house. Cut it small if you want to serve it as an appetizer.

SERVES 6

1 tbsp (15 ml) vegetable oil

1 lb (460 g) tender beef sandwich steaks, raw, thinly sliced

1 green bell pepper, thinly sliced

1 onion, thinly sliced

6 oz (170 g) mushrooms, thinly sliced

1 tbsp (15 ml) Worcestershire sauce

1¼ cups (150 g) self-rising flour, plus more for work surface

1¼ cups (315 g) plain Greek yogurt

8 oz (225 g) provolone cheese, sliced, or substitute shredded mozzarella

2 tbsp (30 g) butter

1 clove garlic, minced

1 tbsp (4 g) minced parsley

Heat the oil in a large skillet over medium-high heat. Add the beef and cook about halfway through, about 3 minutes. Add the bell pepper, onion and mushrooms. Cook for about 7 minutes, or until the meat is cooked through and the vegetables are softened. Add the Worcestershire sauce and stir. Turn off the heat and let it cool slightly.

Preheat the oven to 425°F (220°C) and line a standard baking sheet with parchment paper.

In a medium bowl, combine the flour and yogurt with a wooden spoon, stirring until a sticky dough forms. Generously flour a work surface. Turn dough out onto the work surface and knead, adding a dusting of flour from time to time, until the dough is no longer sticky. Roll or press the dough into a rectangle about 15 x 10 inches (38 x 25 cm). Place the cheese in a long line parallel to the long edge of the dough, leaving a 4-inch (10-cm) margin. Cover the cheese with the beef mixture.

Roll up the dough, cinnamon roll style, until you have a tight cylinder, and pinch the edges shut. Transfer the Stromboli to the prepared baking sheet.

In a small microwaveable dish, heat the butter and garlic until the butter is melted and the garlic is fragrant, about 40 seconds. Add the parsley. Brush the dough with half the butter and garlic mixture. Cut a few slits along the top of the dough to allow steam to escape.

Bake the Stromboli for 14 to 18 minutes, or until it's golden brown. Brush the Stromboli with the remaining butter mixture. Let it cool for 10 minutes before slicing into segments and serving.

CHICKEN AND BUTTERNUT SQUASH POTPIE
WITH SAGE-HERBED CRUST

I dearly love a good chicken potpie on a chilly night. But then I also love to make potpie without any meat at all by leaving out the chicken and adding an extra potato and an extra cup of peas. If ever you have holiday guests that don't eat meat, the vegetarian version makes a special main dish. This potpie could also be made vegan with a few swaps—dairy-free yogurt for the Greek yogurt, olive oil for the butter and cashew cream for the heavy cream.

SERVES 6

CRUST

1¼ cups (150 g) self-rising flour

1¼ cup (315 g) plain Greek yogurt

¼ tsp dried sage

FILLING

2 tbsp (30 g) butter

1 small onion, diced

2 cloves garlic, minced

1 cup (150 g) carrots, chopped

1 large potato, peeled and cut into ½-inch (1.3-cm) pieces

2 cups (280 g) butternut squash, raw, cut into cubes

4 tbsp (35 g) flour

1½ cups (360 ml) chicken broth

2 cups (280 g) chicken or turkey, fully cooked and shredded, or in cubes

1 cup (155 g) peas, defrosted if frozen

½ cup (120 ml) heavy cream or half and half

Salt and pepper

1 egg, beaten

Fresh sage leaves, for garnish

Preheat the oven to 425°F (220°C).

In a large bowl, combine the flour, yogurt and sage. Divide the dough into two equal portions. Roll out one portion of the dough to cover the bottom of a standard pie dish. Place the dough into the pie dish and bake for 10 minutes.

Meanwhile, heat the butter in a large skillet over medium heat. Add the onion, garlic, carrots, potato and squash, stirring often, until the vegetables begin to soften, about 5 minutes. Sprinkle the flour over the vegetables and cook for 2 minutes, stirring often, until the flour is moist and clings to the vegetables. Add the broth and chicken. Bring to a boil, reduce the heat and simmer until the vegetables are cooked through, about 10 minutes. Add the peas and the cream to the pan. Bring the mixture to a simmer. Simmer for 2 minutes, or until the mixture is thickened. Season to taste with salt and pepper.

Pour the mixture into the hot crust in the pie dish. Roll out the remaining dough into a circle to fit over the top of the pie dish. Poke a few holes with a fork in the dough. Brush the crust with the beaten egg. Bake for 14 to 16 minutes, or until the top of the pie is nicely browned and the filling is bubbling up. Let the potpie cool for 10 minutes, and then garnish with sage and serve.

CHINESE BAO WITH PLUM BARBECUE CHICKEN

These cute little dumpling balls have a great balance of flavors—sweet, tangy, salty, savory. You could make a little extra plum BBQ sauce for dipping, like I do. Try the sauce with some edamame, if you have any leftovers. Chinese bao are typically steamed, but I find that the oven works very well to give them a little bit of texture and browning. I like to bake a big batch and then wrap any leftovers individually for freezing. Use any leftover chicken and plum sauce as a quick dinner over white rice.

MAKES 16 DUMPLINGS

4 tbsp (60 ml) Chinese plum sauce

1 tbsp (15 ml) rice wine vinegar

1 tbsp (15 ml) hot mustard or Dijon mustard

1 tbsp (15 ml) soy sauce

3 tbsp (40 g) brown sugar

1 tbsp (15 ml) sesame oil

2 cups (280 g) fully cooked, shredded chicken

½ cup (25 g) scallions, thinly sliced

2 cups (240 g) self-rising flour, plus more for work surface

2 cups (500 g) plain Greek yogurt

1 egg, beaten

¼ cup (40 g) black-and-white sesame seeds

Preheat the oven to 425°F (220°C). Line two baking sheets with parchment paper.

In a medium bowl, combine the plum sauce, vinegar, mustard, soy sauce, brown sugar and sesame oil. Stir in the chicken and scallions.

In a separate large bowl, combine the flour and yogurt, stirring with a wooden spoon until just combined. Generously flour a work surface. Turn out the dough onto the work surface and knead a few times, just until the dough comes together into a ball.

Divide the dough into sixteen equal pieces. Press each piece into a 5-inch (13-cm) diameter circle, dusting with flour as needed to prevent sticking. Pick up a dough round and add a couple of tablespoons of the filling to the center. Gather the dough around the filling and pinch the edges to close. Repeat this process to create sixteen filled bao.

Place the bao on the prepared baking sheets. Brush with egg and sprinkle with sesame seeds. Bake for 14 to 16 minutes, or until they are golden brown. Let them cool for 5 minutes before serving.

CURRIED POTATO AND PEA SAMOSAS

Samosas—vegetable and curry-scented pockets—might be the most flavorful and convenient way to eat your veggies. An authentic samosa should be fried, and you could certainly do that, but I'm happy with healthier baked samosas. Try packing some to go for a memorable lunch. I almost always double or triple this recipe. You'll have extra filling, so you might want to eat it alone, warm, with a big dollop of plain yogurt and mango chutney

MAKES 8 SAMOSAS

1 tbsp (15 g) butter

1 small onion, chopped

1 clove garlic, minced

1 large potato, peeled and diced

1 cup (235 g) cauliflower florets, cut into ½-inch (1.3-cm) pieces

¼ cup (60 ml) water

½ cup (80 g) peas, thawed if frozen

½ tsp salt

1 tbsp (6 g) high-quality curry powder

2 tbsp (30 ml) cream or half and half

1 cup (120 g) self-rising flour, plus more for work surface

1 cup (250 g) plain Greek yogurt

1 egg beaten with 1 tsp curry powder

¼ cup (70 g) mango chutney, for serving

Preheat the oven to 425°F (220°C). Line a baking sheet with parchment paper and set it aside.

In a large skillet, melt the butter over medium heat. Add the onion, garlic, potato and cauliflower and sauté for 5 minutes. Add the water, bring to a boil, cover the skillet with a lid and reduce the heat to simmer for 5 minutes, or until the potatoes are softened. Remove the lid and turn up the heat to medium-high.

Add the peas and cook, just until the water is almost evaporated. Add the salt and curry powder and cook for 30 seconds. Stir in the cream and cook for about 1 minute, or until the cream coats all of the vegetables. Remove the mixture from the heat and let it cool slightly while you prepare the dough.

In a large bowl, stir together the flour and yogurt until just combined. Generously flour a work surface. Turn out the dough onto the work surface and knead just until smooth, adding in more flour to the work surface as needed.

Divide the dough into four pieces. Pat each dough piece into a 6-inch (15-cm) diameter circle, adding more flour to the work surface as needed to prevent sticking. Cut each circle in half. Coat ¼ inch (6 mm) of the rim of the half circle lightly with the beaten egg. Spoon 1 tablespoon (15 g) of the curry mixture onto a dough piece. Fold over to form a cone-shaped samosa. Pinch the edges shut. Place the samosas on the baking sheet. Brush the samosas with the egg/curry powder mixture. Bake for 14 to 16 minutes, or until the samosas are golden brown. Serve with the mango chutney.

THREE-CHEESE EMPANADAS

In my mind, cheese empanadas are a South American version of grilled cheese sandwiches—carbs and cheese. The melty cheese and warm dough are all about comfort food, but they still feel extra special since everything is encased in a portable pocket. When I lived in Santiago, Chile, this was the meal I would most often request. The Chilean cooks would use a small saucer as a size guide for shaping the dough before folding. I'm not that precise, but you could certainly use a guide-dish if you want yours to be as perfect as the Chilean version. One last note: if you don't have all three cheeses on hand, these are perfectly delicious with one flavor of any good melting cheese. I've made these with all mozzarella, all cheddar and all pepper jack with good results.

MAKES 4 EMPANADAS

1 cup (115 g) mozzarella cheese, shredded

½ cup (60 g) provolone cheese, shredded

½ cup (65 g) ricotta cheese

Pinch of crushed red pepper flakes

Freshly ground black pepper

1 cup (120 g) self-rising flour, plus more for work surface

1 cup (250 g) plain Greek yogurt

1 egg, beaten

Preheat the oven to 425°F (220°C). Line a baking sheet with parchment paper.

In a medium bowl, combine the mozzarella, provolone, ricotta, red pepper flakes and lots of freshly ground black pepper.

In a large bowl, stir together the self-rising flour and yogurt until just combined. Generously flour a work surface. Turn out the dough onto the work surface and knead just until smooth, adding in more flour from the work surface as needed. Divide the dough into four pieces. Pat each dough piece into a 6-inch (15-cm) diameter circle, adding more flour to the work surface as needed to prevent sticking. Coat ¼ inch (6 mm) of the rim of the circle lightly with the beaten egg. Add one-fourth of the cheese mixture to one-half of the dough piece. Gently fold the dough over and seal the edges. Repeat the process with the remaining three pieces of dough.

Place the empanadas on the prepared baking sheet. Brush the tops with the remaining beaten egg. Bake for 14 to 16 minutes, or until they are golden brown. Let them cool for 5 minutes before serving.

CHILEAN-STYLE CUMIN-SCENTED BEEF EMPANADAS

These South American–style empanadas are seen at almost every holiday meal in Chile. The filling is just scrumptious and very well balanced with savory meat and heady cumin, salty olives and creamy hardboiled eggs, with a touch of sweetness from the raisins. If you want to make them a little simpler, you can leave out the Chilean additions and just make the meat filling, but they're awfully delicious with all the add-ins.

MAKES 8 EMPANADAS

1 tbsp (15 ml) vegetable oil

1 medium onion, chopped

1 lb (460 g) ground beef, raw

1 tsp cumin

1 tsp paprika

½ tsp garlic powder

½ tsp salt

¼ cup (60 ml) beef broth or water

¼ cup (40 g) raisins

¼ cup (50 g) black olives, chopped

1 hard-boiled egg, coarsely chopped

2 cups (240 g) self-rising flour, plus more for work surface

2 cups (500 g) plain Greek yogurt

1 egg, beaten

Preheat the oven to 425°F (220°C). Line a baking sheet with parchment paper and set it aside.

In a large skillet over medium heat, warm the vegetable oil. Add the onion and ground beef and cook, breaking up the beef with the back of a spoon until the meat is no longer pink, about 8 minutes. Add the cumin, paprika, garlic powder and salt and stir for 30 seconds. Stir in the beef broth, raisins, olives and hard-boiled egg. Gently stir the mixture together. Remove the mixture from the heat and allow it to cool briefly while you make the dough.

In a large bowl, using a wooden spoon, combine the flour and yogurt until just combined. Generously flour a work surface. Turn out the dough onto the work surface and divide into eight equal pieces. Press each piece into a 6-inch (15-cm) diameter circle, adding more flour as necessary to prevent sticking. Spread a little beaten egg around the edges of the circles. Add one-eighth of the meat mixture to each empanada and fold over to create a pocket, pinching the edges to seal. Don't worry if the empanadas tear a little while you are working with the dough; they will still come out just fine.

Brush the finished empanadas with the beaten egg and bake for 14 to 16 minutes, or until they are golden brown. Allow them to cool for 5 minutes before serving.

BUFFALO CHICKEN AND BLUE CHEESE POCKETS

I once won a recipe contest with a prize package that included a whole case of red hot sauce. I wasn't sure what I was going to do with all those bottles, but my kids quickly took over, pouring it onto quesadillas, grilled cheese sandwiches, eggs, tacos, hamburgers and more. The bottles were gone in no time. Now I have to buy my hot sauce to make these fun and yummy chicken and blue cheese pockets, with a little surprise creaminess from the addition of cream cheese, just to keep the heat in balance. If you have leftover chicken after making the pockets, stir it into some warm cream cheese for a hot buffalo dip.

SERVES 4

2 cups (280 g) chicken, shredded

1 tbsp (15 ml) butter, melted

¼ cup (60 ml) hot sauce

2 tbsp (6 g) scallions, chopped

Salt and pepper

1 cup (120 g) self-rising flour, plus more for work surface

1 cup (250 g) plain Greek yogurt

3 oz (85 g) cream cheese

¼ cup (30 g) blue cheese, crumbled

1 egg, beaten

1 tbsp (9 g) poppy seeds

Celery sticks, for serving

Blue cheese dressing, for serving

Preheat the oven to 425°F (220°C). Line a baking sheet with parchment paper.

In a medium bowl, combine the chicken, butter, hot sauce and scallions. Season to taste with salt and pepper.

In a large bowl, combine the flour and yogurt into a sticky dough. Generously flour a work surface. Turn out the dough onto the work surface and knead a few times, until the dough is smooth. Divide the dough into four equal pieces. Roll or press each piece into a 6- or 7-inch (15- or 18-cm) diameter circle, adding more flour as needed to prevent sticking.

Spread one-fourth of the cream cheese onto one side of the dough circle. Sprinkle with a tablespoon (7 g) of the blue cheese and about ½ cup (70 g) of the chicken mixture. Fold up the dough to form a semicircle pocket. Close the edges by adding a little of the beaten egg to just the rim and pressing down with a fork. Repeat the process with all four pockets.

Place the prepared pockets on the baking sheet and brush with the beaten egg. Poke the tops with a fork a few times for letting out the steam. Sprinkle with the poppy seeds and bake for about 16 to 18 minutes, or until the pockets are nicely browned. Let the pockets cool for 10 minutes before serving. Serve with the traditional celery sticks and blue cheese dressing.

GRILLED MOROCCAN CHICKEN AND VEGETABLE FLATBREAD

Here's a meal that can be made entirely outdoors. It's great for an at-home dinner in the summer when you don't feel like turning on the oven. Most of the components can be made well in advance, keeping the workload to a minimum and the delicious payoff at a maximum.

SERVES 4

Special equipment: metal skewers or wooden skewers that have been soaked in water for 30 minutes prior to grilling

½ tsp cumin

¼ tsp red chili flakes

½ tsp turmeric

1 tsp paprika

Pinch of ground cinnamon

1 tbsp (15 g) brown sugar

1 lb (460 g) chicken, raw, cut into 1-inch (2.5-cm) pieces

3 tbsp (45 ml) olive oil, divided

Juice of ½ lemon

1 red onion, cut into 1-inch (2.5-cm) pieces

1 zucchini, ends trimmed, cut into ½-inch (1.3-cm) rings

1 cup (120 g) self-rising flour, plus more for work surface

1¾ cups (335 g) plain Greek yogurt, divided

2 tbsp (30 ml) lemon juice

2 tbsp (4 g) cilantro, chopped, plus more leaves for serving

Salt and pepper

For the chicken, in a small bowl, combine the cumin, chili flakes, turmeric, paprika, cinnamon and brown sugar. Place half of the mixture into a zip-top bag. Add the chicken, 2 tablespoons (30 ml) of olive oil and lemon juice. Let the chicken marinate for at least 20 minutes and up to 4 hours.

Preheat a grill to high. Thread the chicken on a skewer, alternating with onion and zucchini pieces.

Meanwhile, for the flatbread, in a large bowl, combine the flour and 1 cup (250 g) of yogurt with a wooden spoon. Turn out the dough onto a generously floured work surface. Knead a few times until the dough is no longer sticky. Divide the dough into four equal portions. Roll or press each dough piece into an oval about 8 inches (20 cm) long. Brush both sides of the dough with the remaining tablespoon (15 ml) olive oil. Place the dough on the grill and cook for about 2 minutes per side, or until the dough is blackened in a few places but is cooked through. Stack the flatbreads on a plate and set aside, covered. Grill the chicken and vegetables to your liking, about 15 minutes, turning often.

For the yogurt sauce, in a small bowl, combine the remaining yogurt, lemon juice, cilantro and remaining spice mixture. Season the mixture to taste with salt and pepper. To serve, pass the flatbreads to be filled with yogurt sauce, chicken/vegetable skewers and additional cilantro leaves.

GEORGIAN CHEESE AND EGG BREAD—KHACHAPURI

These little cheese and egg boats are a national food of the country Georgia. In fact, *khachapuri* means cheese bread. They make a stunning presentation, especially when you see several of them together. The proper way to eat khachapuri is to keep the egg on the runny side—even the whites—and then mix it up a little with the hot cheese filling, pulling away pieces of the bread crust to dip in the cheese and egg mixture. Any way you eat it, it's going to be absolutely delicious.

SERVES 4

1 cup (120 g) self-rising flour, plus more for work surface

1 cup (250 g) Greek yogurt

2 cups (230 g) mozzarella cheese, shredded

2 oz (60 g) feta cheese, crumbled

1 egg, beaten

4 eggs, for inside each khachapuri

1 tbsp (15 g) butter

Salt and pepper

Parsley, for garnish

Preheat the oven to 400°F (200°C). Line a baking sheet with parchment paper and set aside.

In a large bowl, combine the flour and yogurt with a wooden spoon until just combined. Generously flour a work surface. Turn out the dough onto the work surface and knead a few times, just until a smooth dough forms. Divide the dough into four pieces. Press each dough piece into a 6-inch (15-cm) circle. Fold up the edges of the circle to create a rim and stretch the dough into a canoe shape. Don't be too picky! There are a lot of different shapes for khachapuri and none of them are wrong.

In a separate medium bowl, combine the mozzarella and feta cheese. Fill the insides of the canoe-shaped dough with the cheese mixture, dividing evenly. Brush the outsides of the dough with the beaten egg. Place on the prepared baking sheet.

Bake the khachapuri for 10 to 12 minutes, or until the edges begin to brown. Remove them from the oven. Using the back of the spoon, make an indentation in the center of the cheese filling. Crack an egg into the center of each khachapuri. Dot the cheese with a little butter on each khachapuri and season with salt and pepper. Return the khachapuri to the oven for 4 to 5 minutes, or until the egg is a little set, but still jiggly in the yolk and surrounding whites. Remove them from the oven. Sprinkle them with parsley and serve immediately.

NOTES: Stir the egg into the cheese mixture so that the egg continues to cook. If you'd like to serve without stirring in the egg mixture, just bake the khachapuri a little longer until the whites are set.

ENGLISH BEEF AND POTATO HAND PIE "PASTIES"

My great-grandmother was from England. She was a remarkable seamstress and cook. My dad fondly remembers the little meat pies she used to make, pasties or Cornish pasties as they are called. These meat pies will stick to your ribs and warm you through and through with their meat and potato goodness. Any extra filling would also be nice stuffed in a roasted red bell pepper half.

MAKES 8

1 tbsp (15 ml) vegetable oil

1 onion, diced

1 large russet potato, peeled and diced

½ lb (115 g) ground beef, raw

½ lb (115 g) ground pork, raw

⅓ cup (80 ml) beef stock

½ cup (80 g) frozen peas, optional

½ tsp dried thyme

½ tsp dried sage

½ tsp salt

2 cups (240 g) self-rising flour, plus more for work surface

2 cups (500 g) plain Greek yogurt

1 egg, beaten

Preheat the oven to 425°F (220°C). Line a baking sheet with parchment paper and set aside.

In a large skillet over medium heat, warm the vegetable oil. Add the onion and potato and cook, breaking up for about 5 minutes, or until the onion begins to soften. Add the ground beef and pork and continue to cook, breaking up the meat with the back of a wooden spoon, until the meat is no longer pink, about 8 minutes. Add the stock, peas, thyme, sage and salt. Cover and simmer until the potatoes are softened, about 5 minutes. Remove the mixture from the heat and allow it to cool briefly while you make the dough.

In a large bowl, combine the flour and yogurt with a wooden spoon until just combined. Generously flour a work surface. Turn out the dough onto the work surface and divide it into eight equal pieces. Press each piece into a 6-inch (15-cm) diameter circle, adding more flour as necessary to prevent sticking. Spread a little beaten egg around the edges of the circles. Add one-eighth of the meat mixture to each dough circle and fold over to create a pocket, pinching the edges to seal. Don't worry if the dough tears a little while you are working with the dough. They will still come out just fine.

Brush the finished pastries with the beaten egg and bake for 14 to 16 minutes, or until they are golden brown. Allow them to cool for 5 minutes before serving.

PIZZA BIANCO-STYLE FIG, PROSCIUTTO AND CHEESE SANDWICHES

In Rome, you can buy slabs of very thin, flat pizza that can be folded over into sandwiches for portable eating. This recipe is inspired by one of my favorite flavor combinations—fig, cheese and prosciutto. If figs are out of season, a slice of melon or pear would also be lovely here.

SERVES 4

1½ cups (180 g) self-rising flour, plus more for work surface

1½ cups (375 g) plain Greek yogurt

1 tbsp (15 ml) olive oil

¾ cup (95 g) ricotta cheese

1½ cups (175 g) mozzarella cheese, shredded

¼ cup (45 g) Parmesan cheese, grated

Salt and pepper

6 oz (180 g) prosciutto, thinly sliced

6 small fresh figs, sliced into ⅓-inch (0.8-cm) rings

1 cup (75 g) arugula tossed with 1 tbsp (15 ml) olive oil

1 tbsp (15 ml) balsamic glaze (see note)

Preheat the oven to 425°F (220°C). Line a standard-sized baking sheet with parchment paper and coat it lightly with cooking spray.

In a large bowl, combine the flour, yogurt and olive oil with a wooden spoon. Generously flour a work surface. Turn out the dough onto the work surface and knead a few times until a smooth dough forms. Place the dough onto the prepared baking sheet and press the dough until it reaches the edges.

In a medium bowl, combine the ricotta, mozzarella and Parmesan cheese. Season with salt and pepper and spread onto the prepared dough. Bake the pizza for about 14 to 16 minutes, or until the edges are browned and the cheese is bubbly. Immediately top with prosciutto and figs. Return to the oven and bake for 1 minute. Let the pizza cool for 5 minutes. Scatter the arugula over the top of the pizza and drizzle with the balsamic glaze. Slice the pizza horizontally into four equal pieces. Fold over each pizza section into a sandwich. Serve immediately.

NOTE: A balsamic glaze is balsamic vinegar and sweetener reduced to a thick syrup. You can purchase balsamic glaze in the grocery store, but if you'd like to make your own, just simmer 1 cup (240 ml) of balsamic vinegar and ¼ cup (60 g) of brown sugar until thick and syrupy, about 18 minutes.

OCTOBERFEST CHEESY MUSTARD-WRAPPED BRATS

I started making our own family Octoberfest dinner years ago. To make this a little easier to execute, I usually make bratwurst and roasted apples and potatoes a few nights before, setting aside four bratwursts for the wrapped brats a few nights later. If you've got fully cooked bratwurst, the rest comes together in a snap!

SERVES 4

1 cup (120 g) self-rising flour, plus more for work surface

1 cup (250 g) plain Greek yogurt

4 bratwurst sausages, fully cooked and cooled

4 oz (115 g) Muenster or cheddar cheese, cut into small thin pieces

2 tbsp (32 g) stone ground mustard

½ cup (75 g) sauerkraut, well-drained, optional

1 egg, beaten

1 tbsp (7 g) caraway seeds

Preheat the oven to 425°F (220°C). Line a baking sheet with foil or parchment paper.

In a medium bowl, combine the flour and yogurt with a wooden spoon, just until it begins to come together into a ball. Generously flour a work surface. Turn out the dough onto the work surface and knead a few times, just until the mixture comes together into a smooth ball. Divide the dough into four equal pieces. Press each piece into a 5 x 3-inch (13 x 8-cm) circle, dusting with flour as needed to prevent sticking.

Place a bratwurst in the center of each dough round. Make a few 1-inch (2.5-cm) slices into each bratwurst, not cutting all the way through to the bottom. Poke in pieces of the cheese. Cover the top of the bratwurst with a little mustard and a little sauerkraut, if you're using. Roll up the dough around the bratwurst. The ends of the bratwurst should be sticking out a little.

Place the brats on the prepared baking sheet. Brush with egg and sprinkle with the caraway seeds. Bake for 14 to 17 minutes, or until the dough is golden brown. Let them cool for 5 minutes before serving.

TEXAS CHORIZO AND PICKLED JALAPEÑO KOLACHES

These kolaches are inspired by the big tasty buns you find all over Texas. Kolaches can be sweet or savory, but this Lone Star State version is savory and, in true Texas style, a bit spicy. If you want to turn down the heat, use less jalapeño and switch your cheese to plain jack or cheddar. You could also use leftover taco meat for the chorizo, if you've got extra on hand.

MAKES 4 KOLACHES

1 cup (120 g) self-rising flour, plus more for work surface

1 cup (250 g) plain Greek yogurt

2 tbsp (30 g) butter, grated

½ tsp sugar

1 egg, beaten

½ cup (70 g) pepper jack cheese, shredded, plus more for the tops of the rolls

1 cup (150 g) chorizo, cooked, crumbled

¼ cup (30 g) pickled jalapeño slices

Preheat the oven to 425°F (220°C). Line a baking sheet with parchment paper.

In a medium bowl, combine the flour, yogurt, butter and sugar. Generously flour a work surface. Turn out the dough onto the work surface and knead it a few times, just until the mixture develops into a smooth ball. Divide the dough into four equal sections. Shape each section into a ball. Push your finger through the center of the ball, as if to make a bagel. Repeat the process with all of the dough sections. Place each roll on the prepared baking sheet and brush with the beaten egg.

Sprinkle the cheese into the hole of each roll. Divide the chorizo and jalapeños between each of the rolls, placing into the center of the rolls on top of the cheese. Add a little sprinkle of cheese to the top of the chorizo and jalapeño. Bake for 16 to 18 minutes, or until the rolls are golden brown. Let the kolaches cool for 5 minutes before serving.

SPINACH, GRUYÈRE AND BACON QUICHE

I love to make quiche when I can't quite figure out what to make for breakfast, lunch or dinner. Quiche can be made with a handful of fresh ingredients. Even though quiche has a throw-together quality, it's still spiffy enough for company. This version is much lighter than traditional heavy, butter and cream quiches, but it's still every bit as delicious.

SERVES 6

⅔ cup (80 g) self-rising flour, plus more for work surface

⅔ cup (170 g) plain Greek yogurt

1–2 tbsp (15–30 ml) butter, melted, use the greater amount for a richer, more tender crust

1 tbsp (15 ml) olive oil

½ red onion, diced

2 cups (460 g) baby spinach, stems removed

3 eggs

1 cup (240 ml) whole milk

½ tsp salt

¼ tsp pepper

1 cup (135 g) Gruyère cheese, grated

8 slices bacon, cooked crisp and crumbled

Preheat the oven to 425°F (220°C). Coat a pie or quiche dish with nonstick cooking spray.

In a medium bowl, combine the flour, yogurt and melted butter until just combined. Turn out the dough onto a floured surface and give it a couple of kneads, just until a smooth dough forms. Press the dough into the pie dish. Bake for 8 minutes, or until the crust is just beginning to be set.

While the crust bakes, in a medium skillet, heat the oil over medium heat. Add the onion and sauté until it just begins to soften, about 4 minutes. Add the spinach and sauté until just wilted, about 90 seconds.

In a separate medium bowl, beat the eggs, milk, salt and pepper until fully combined.

When the crust comes out of the oven, scatter the onion/spinach mixture, cheese and bacon over the crust. Pour the egg mixture over the top and return to the oven.

Bake for 18 to 22 minutes, or until the eggs are puffed and set. Let the quiche cool for 5 minutes and serve. The quiche can be served at room temperature also.

SWEETS AND TREATS

It might be hard to believe, but two-ingredient dough can be the base of delicious desserts too. It takes a few more ingredients to pull it all together, but using yogurt and self-rising flour as the base for treats makes them a little bit easier and a little healthier also. You'll find everything you need to get started on making quick sweet rolls, donuts, waffles, cobblers, cakes—including my favorite chocolate version—and more.

RASPBERRY-ORANGE BREAKFAST ROLLS

Of course you already love cinnamon rolls. Who doesn't? These are extra-special cousins of cinnamon rolls. You won't find cinnamon here, although you could add some, if you'd like. Instead, you'll find a tender, buttery roll with spirals of raspberry jam and a coating of sunshine in the form of a shiny orange glaze. My mother used to make a variation of these rolls on Christmas Eve to celebrate not just the coming of Christmas but also my sister's December 24th birthday.

MAKES 12

ROLLS

1 cup (250 g) vanilla-flavored Greek yogurt

1¼ cups (210 g) self-rising flour, plus more for the work surface

1 tbsp (10 g) orange zest

2 tbsp (30 g) cold butter

4 tbsp (80 g) raspberry jam

GLAZE

1 cup (135 g) powdered sugar

3 tbsp (45 ml) freshly squeezed orange juice, plus more if needed

Fresh raspberries, for garnish

Preheat the oven to 425°F (220°C). Lightly grease a standard pie dish. I like to use an aluminum pie pan.

In a medium bowl, combine the yogurt, flour and orange zest with a wooden spoon to form a sticky ball. Using a box grater, shred the butter into the dough. You can also cut it into tiny pieces with a knife, if you'd rather. Stir the butter into the dough until just combined.

Prepare a work surface by coating it generously with flour. Turn out the dough onto the work surface. Knead for 1 minute, allowing the dough to absorb the flour from the work surface, until the dough is smooth. Roll or pat the dough into a rough rectangle, about 12 x 7 inches (30 x 18 cm). Spread the dough with the raspberry jam, coming almost all the way to the edges. Roll up the dough, starting with the long edge, into a cylinder shape, pinching the dough to close. Cut the dough crosswise into twelve spiral-shaped rolls. The dough will be tender. If it squishes or tears a bit, just gently press it back into shape. It will still be delicious!

Place the rolls into the prepared pan. The rolls will be touching in places. Bake the rolls for about 20 minutes, or until nicely browned on top with the jam bubbling up. Let the rolls cool for at least 10 minutes before glazing.

For the glaze, in a small bowl, combine the powdered sugar and orange juice, stirring until smooth. Frost the warm rolls with the beautiful orange glaze. Garnish with fresh raspberries.

MAPLE-PECAN STICKY BUNS

I bought three bottles of pure maple syrup on a recent trip to Vermont—only I forgot to pack them in my suitcase and left them in my carry-on. They never made it through airport security. I had to leave my souvenir syrup with the airport security agent. Bye-bye, Vermont maple syrup. As soon as I got home, I went to my local grocery store in Utah, determined to get some maple syrup. I found the same brand I bought on vacation, and the price was even a little cheaper! You should know that I always overpay for everything on vacation. Whenever I've got real maple syrup on hand, these are my go-to rolls.

MAKES 12

TOPPING

1 cup (125 g) pecan pieces

¼ cup (60 g) butter

½ cup (115 g) dark brown sugar, packed

¼ cup (60 ml) pure maple syrup, B grade preferred

DOUGH

1¼ cups (150 g) self-rising flour, plus more for work surface

1 cup (250 g) vanilla-flavored Greek yogurt

1 tbsp (15 ml) butter, melted

3 tbsp (40 g) sugar

FILLING

1 tbsp (15 g) butter, softened

½ cup (115 g) dark brown sugar, packed

2 tbsp (25 g) granulated sugar

2 tsp (5 g) ground cinnamon

Preheat the oven to 425°F (220°C). Coat a glass pie dish with butter.

For the topping, scatter the pecans onto the bottom of the pie dish. In a medium microwave-safe bowl, melt the butter. Add the brown sugar and maple syrup, stirring until it's well combined. Pour the maple syrup mixture over the pecans. Set the pie dish aside.

For the dough, in a medium bowl, combine the flour, yogurt, melted butter and sugar. Generously flour a work surface. Transfer the dough to the work surface and knead a few times, just until the dough develops into a ball, kneading in more flour so the dough isn't too sticky to work with. Roll or press the dough into a rectangle, about 12 x 7 inches (30 x 18 cm).

For the filling, spread the softened butter onto the dough and sprinkle evenly with the brown sugar, granulated sugar and cinnamon.

Starting with the long end, roll up the dough into a cylinder, pinching the ends to shut. Cut the dough into twelve rolls and place, evenly spaced, in the prepared pie dish. Some of the rolls will be touching.

Bake the rolls for about 18 minutes, or until they are golden brown on the tops. Immediately place a heat-proof plate on top of the pie dish. Using oven mitts, grasp the pie dish and turn it over so that the rolls come off onto the plate. They should be topped with pecans and a beautiful maple glaze.

Let the rolls cool for about 5 minutes, or until you can manage that gorgeous syrup without burning your mouth. I usually start eating the rolls at around the 4-minute mark.

CINNAMON-CARDAMOM BRAID

You can make this any time of year, of course, but it looks especially pretty and festive at Christmastime. I like to make this as a drop-off gift for my neighbors, wrapped in cellophane and trimmed with red ribbon and pine sprigs.

SERVES 6

DOUGH

1½ cups (180 g) self-rising flour, plus more for work surface

1 cup (250 g) vanilla-flavored Greek yogurt

2 tbsp (30 ml) butter, melted

1 egg

2 tbsp (25 g) sugar

FILLING

2 tbsp (30 ml) butter, melted

½ cup (115 g) dark brown sugar

2 tbsp (25 g) granulated sugar

1 tsp ground cinnamon

1 tsp cardamom

ICING

¾ cup (100 g) powdered sugar

½ tsp vanilla extract

2 tbsp (30 ml) cream or milk

Preheat the oven to 425°F (220°C). Line a baking sheet with parchment paper.

For the dough, in a medium bowl, combine the flour, yogurt, melted butter, egg and sugar until the mixture forms a shaggy dough. Generously flour a work surface. Transfer the dough to the work surface and knead, just until the dough develops into a smooth ball. Press or roll the dough into a 12 x 7-inch (30 x 18–cm) rectangle.

For the filling, in a small bowl combine the melted butter, brown sugar, granulated sugar, cinnamon and cardamom. Spread the filling over the dough. Roll the dough into a cylinder, starting with the long edge. Using sharp scissors, cut the dough into three vertical strands, not cutting all the way to the top, so that the three stands are still connected at the top. Braid the strands together and then transfer the braid to the prepared baking sheet.

Bake for about 20 to 22 minutes, or until the dough is golden brown. Remove it from the oven and allow the braid to cool for 10 minutes.

For the icing, combine the powdered sugar, vanilla and cream to form a very thick glaze. Drizzle the icing over the still-warm braid.

LEMON CREAM CHEESE BREAKFAST PASTRIES

These are the sunniest little sweeties that will ever grace your breakfast table. I'll choose a lemon breakfast pastry over any other flavor every time. The lemon curd and the cream cheese keep these from being overly sugary, so the pastry is balanced with creamy, puckery-tart and sweet flavors. You'll have extra cream cheese filling. I like to give everyone a little dollop of extra filling on the side to enjoy with the pastry.

MAKES 8

1½ cups (180 g) self-rising flour, plus more for work surface

1 cup (250 g) vanilla-flavored Greek yogurt

3 oz (85 g) cream cheese, softened

3 tbsp (45 g) sugar, divided

½ tsp vanilla extract

1 egg

¼ cup (65 g) lemon curd

Preheat the oven to 425°F (220°C). Line a baking sheet with parchment paper and set aside.

In a medium bowl, combine the flour and yogurt with a wooden spoon, mixing until a rough, shaggy dough forms. Generously dust a work surface with flour. Turn out the dough onto the work surface and knead it a few times, until the dough forms a smooth ball, about 1 minute. Cut the dough into eight equal-sized pieces. Roll each piece into a ball and flatten to about 3 inches (8 cm) in diameter. Place on the prepared baking sheet. Using the back of a spoon, dipped in flour, make an indentation in the center of each dough circle.

In a small bowl, combine the cream cheese, 2 tablespoons (30 g) of sugar and vanilla. Brush the dough circles all over with egg. Fill each dough center with about a tablespoon (15 g) of the cream cheese mixture.

Top the cream cheese mixture with a generous dollop, about 1 large rounded teaspoon, of the lemon curd. Sprinkle the outside of the pastries with the remaining 1 tablespoon (15 g) of sugar.

Bake the pastries for about 15 to 18 minutes, or until they are golden brown. Let them cool for 5 minutes before serving.

FRENCH TOAST CINNAMON AND MAPLE BITES

For a short time, we had a made-to-order donut place in our small town. The lines were long, the process was slow, but the donuts were delicious. I always requested a donut with a maple glaze and a cinnamon-sugar topping. The flavor of cinnamon sugar with maple always tastes like French toast to me. These stuffed bagels are a nod to those favorite donuts of mine.

MAKES 6

DOUGH

1 cup (120 g) self-rising flour, plus more for work surface

1 cup (250 g) nonfat Greek yogurt

¼ tsp nutmeg

FILLING

4 oz (115 g) cream cheese, softened

2 tbsp (30 ml) pure maple syrup

TOPPING

2 tbsp (30 ml) butter, melted

2 tbsp (25 g) granulated sugar

½ tsp ground cinnamon

Preheat the oven to 425°F (220°C). Line a baking sheet with parchment paper and set aside.

For the dough, in a medium bowl, using a wooden spoon, combine the flour, yogurt and nutmeg until a shaggy dough forms. Generously flour a work surface. Transfer the dough to the work surface and knead it a few times until it becomes smooth. Divide the dough into six equal pieces; roll each piece into a ball and flatten slightly into a disk. Set the disks aside to make the filling.

For the filling, in a small bowl combine the cream cheese and maple syrup. Using a teaspoon, scoop one-sixth of the cream cheese mixture into a small ball. Place the cream cheese ball in the center of a dough disk and bring the edges of the dough around the cream cheese to enclose. Turn the bagel ball over so that the seam side is down and place the ball on the prepared baking sheet. Repeat the process with the remaining dough.

For the topping, brush the dough balls with the melted butter. In a small bowl, combine the sugar and cinnamon. Sprinkle the dough balls generously with the cinnamon-sugar mixture and bake for 18 to 20 minutes, or until they are golden brown. Let the bagel balls cool for 5 minutes before eating. The cream cheese will be very hot, so use caution.

BLUEBERRY-LEMON VISITING LOAF

I don't have an afternoon teatime tradition, but if I did, I imagine this sweet little loaf would be the perfect midday treat. It's such a pretty loaf, studded with blueberries and glazed with creamy lemon icing. It just seems to be meant for sharing with a good friend. Maybe make two loaves so you have one to deliver to a neighbor who needs a reason to smile.

SERVES 6

LOAF

1½ cups (180 g) self-rising flour, plus more for work surface

1 cup (250 g) vanilla-flavored Greek yogurt

1 egg

4 tbsp (50 g) sugar

2 tbsp (30 ml) butter, melted

2 tsp (6 g) lemon zest

¾ cup (75 g) blueberries, fresh or frozen

ICING

½ cup (70 g) powdered sugar

1 tbsp (15 g) butter, softened

1 tbsp (15 ml) cream or milk, plus more if needed

1 tbsp (15 ml) lemon juice

Preheat the oven to 425°F (220°C). Line a baking sheet with parchment paper.

For the loaf, in a large bowl, using a wooden spoon, combine the flour, yogurt, egg, sugar, melted butter and lemon zest. Gently stir in the blueberries.

Generously flour a work surface. Turn out the dough onto the floured surface and gently knead a few times until the dough is smooth. Some of the blueberries might get a little smashed, and that's just fine. Flatten the dough into a 7-inch (18-cm) round disk. Cut a giant X on the top of the dough.

Transfer the loaf to the baking sheet and bake for 20 to 22 minutes, or until the loaf is golden brown and the inside cracks of the X are dry to the touch. Remove the loaf from the oven and let it cool for 10 minutes.

For the icing, combine the powdered sugar, softened butter, cream and lemon juice until smooth, adding more cream if needed. Spoon the icing over the warm loaf. You can let the icing set and package the loaf prettily to bring to a friend, or you can cut yourself a big wedge and invite a friend to come to you.

NEW YORK–STYLE CRUMB COFFEE CAKE

At our house, this is the most requested birthday breakfast. I like to stir the coffee cake together the night before and put it in the fridge until the morning. All I have to do is pop it in the oven, and the birthday boy or girl gets a delicious slice of warm coffee cake before school begins. Like all good New York–style coffee cakes, this has a thin layer of batter and a fat layer of crumb. Be sure to tightly wrap up any leftovers to prevent it from drying out.

SERVES 12

CAKE

Butter for greasing the pan

1½ cups (180 g) self-rising flour

1 cup (250 g) vanilla-flavored Greek yogurt

2 tbsp (25 g) granulated sugar

2 tbsp (30 ml) vegetable oil

1 egg

½ tsp vanilla extract

CRUMB TOPPING

½ cup (120 ml) butter, melted and cooled slightly

1¼ cups (150 g) all-purpose flour

¾ cup (170 g) brown sugar

1 tsp ground cinnamon

Powdered sugar, for garnish

Preheat the oven to 425°F (220°C). Grease a 9 x 13-inch (23 x 33-cm) glass baking dish with butter.

For the cake, in a medium bowl, combine the self-rising flour, yogurt, sugar, oil, egg and vanilla with a wooden spoon, stirring just until a sticky batter forms with no dry spots.

Using wet fingers, press the thick batter into the prepared baking dish, wetting fingers as often as necessary to form a thin layer of batter that stretches all across the pan. This will take a little patience, since the batter will be thinly stretched, but just keep working on it until you get the batter to all four corners. Bake the batter for 10 minutes.

For the crumb topping, in a medium bowl, combine the butter, all-purpose flour, brown sugar and cinnamon. Remove the batter from the oven after 10 minutes. Using your fingers, crumble the topping all over the surface of the half-baked batter. Return the coffee cake to the oven and bake for 12 minutes, or until the topping is set and golden brown in places. Let the coffee cake cool for 10 minutes. Sprinkle with powdered sugar.

CINI-MINI CHURROS WITH MILK CHOCOLATE DIPPING SAUCE

Whenever I travel to Mexico or Spain, one of the first things I do is hunt down a churro. In Mexico, you can find churros that are stuffed with fudgy chocolate, but in Spain, churros are dipped into a rich ganache-like chocolate sauce. These churros are so fast and easy, you can virtually transport yourself to a churro shop in less than 30 minutes.

MAKES 12

1 cup (120 g) self-rising flour, plus more for work surface

1 cup (250 g) plain Greek yogurt

1 tbsp (15 ml) butter, melted

½ cup + 2 tbsp (125 g) granulated sugar, divided

1 tsp ground cinnamon

Oil for frying

½ cup (120 ml) heavy cream

3 oz (85 g) milk chocolate, chopped

Line a plate with paper towels.

In a medium bowl, using a wooden spoon, combine the flour, yogurt, butter and 2 tablespoons (25 g) of sugar. Stir until a shaggy dough forms. Generously flour a work surface. Turn out the dough onto the work surface and knead until smooth. Divide the dough into four equal sections. Roll each section into a 12-inch (30-cm) snake. Cut each snake into three pieces. You'll have twelve pieces total.

In a small bowl, combine the ½ cup (100 g) of granulated sugar and cinnamon and set aside.

Heat 1 inch (2.5 cm) of oil in a small pot until the oil reaches 340°F (170°C). Carefully lower three or four dough sections into the oil and fry until they are golden brown, turning once, about 30 seconds per side. Remove them from the oil and drain on the paper towel–lined plate. Repeat the process with the remaining dough sections. While still hot, toss the fried churros in the cinnamon-sugar mixture to coat.

Meanwhile, in a small, microwaveable dish, microwave the cream until it just starts to boil, about 45 seconds. Add the chocolate to the hot cream, cover and let stand for 2 minutes. Whisk the chocolate mixture with a fork until smooth. Serve the hot churros with milk chocolate ganache.

LEMON AND VANILLA
ITALIAN DONUTS—CASTAGNOLE

You'll find these little donut balls in Italy at Carnival time, usually just before Lent. I like to pile a few of them into a paper cone for serving. I always deliver some of these fresh little donuts to my mother—who also happens to be my neighbor—because she loves them so much.

MAKES ABOUT 16

¾ cup + 2 tbsp (175 g) granulated sugar, divided, for rolling the donut balls

1 egg

1½ cups (180 g) self-rising flour

1 tbsp (15 ml) butter, melted

1 cup (250 g) plain Greek yogurt

1 tsp vanilla extract

1 tsp lemon zest

Oil to come up 2 inches (5 cm) in a heavy-bottomed saucepan

Line a plate with paper towels. Put the ¾ cup (150 g) of sugar into a small bowl or pie plate.

In a medium bowl, beat the egg and 2 tablespoons (25 g) of sugar until it's pale yellow. Stir in the flour, butter, yogurt, vanilla and zest. Shape the dough into 1-inch (2.5-cm) balls, flouring your hands as needed.

Meanwhile, heat the oil to 350°F (180°C). Working in batches, fry the donut balls until they are golden brown, flipping once to brown both sides. Remove the donuts to the paper towel–lined plate and immediately roll in the sugar. Serve warm.

RASPBERRY-FILLED JELLY DONUT HOLES

Jelly donuts are a childhood, school-yard favorite for me, even though the powdered sugar used to always make me cough and sputter. Maybe that was part of the fun of eating donuts on the playground with friends.

MAKES ABOUT 16

Special equipment: pastry bag with medium-sized piping tip

1 cup (135 g) powdered sugar

1 egg

2 tbsp (25 g) granulated sugar

1 tbsp (15 ml) butter, melted

1½ cup (180 g) self-rising flour

1 cup (250 g) plain Greek yogurt

Oil to come up 2 inches (5 cm) in a heavy-bottomed saucepan

½ cup (160 g) raspberry jelly

Line a plate with paper towels. Place the powdered sugar in a wide bowl for rolling the donuts.

In a medium bowl, whisk the egg and granulated sugar until pale yellow. Gently stir in the butter. Stir in the flour and yogurt and mix just until combined. Shape the dough into 1-inch (2.5-cm) balls, flouring your hands as needed to prevent sticking.

Heat the oil over medium-high heat until it reaches 350°F (180°C). Working in batches, fry the donuts until they are golden brown, turning once. Remove the donuts to the paper towel–lined plate. Roll the donuts in the powdered sugar.

Fill a pastry bag fitted with a medium-sized piping tip with the jelly. Insert the tip halfway into the donut and pipe a bit of jam into each donut. Serve the donuts warm, and be careful not to cough.

SWEET IRISH SODA BREAD WITH CURRANTS AND RAISINS

I'm duty bound to make this special bread for St. Patrick's Day every year, but it would be wonderful any day, especially if you serve it warm with a generous dollop of creamy Irish butter. You can add caraway seeds if you like for an interesting sweet and savory twist, but I like it best with dried fruit and a crunchy sugar topping.

SERVES 8

½ cup (80 g) dried currants or dried cranberries

¼ cup (40 g) raisins

1½ cups (180 g) self-rising flour, plus more for work surface

1 cup (250 g) vanilla-flavored Greek yogurt

4 tbsp (50 g) sugar

1 egg

2 tbsp (30 g) cold butter, grated

2 tbsp (30 ml) cream or milk

2 tbsp (35 g) turbinado or coarse sugar

Place the currants and raisins in a small dish and cover with 1 cup (240 ml) boiling water. Set aside for 10 minutes.

Meanwhile, line a baking sheet with parchment paper and preheat the oven to 425°F (220°C).

In a medium bowl, combine the flour, yogurt, sugar, egg and butter. Drain the currants and raisins and stir them into the dough.

Generously flour a work surface. Turn out the dough onto the work surface. Knead the dough until a smooth dough forms, about 1 minute. Place the dough on the prepared baking sheet and brush with the cream and sprinkle with the turbinado.

Using a sharp knife, score the bread into eight pieces, cutting pie style into wedges, but not cutting all the way through to the bottom. Bake for 22 to 24 minutes, or until it's golden brown. Serve in wedges with whipped butter if you like.

PINEAPPLE AND COCONUT KOLACHES

This is a fun, tropical-inspired twist on the Czech pastry that has become a Texas staple. This version has a lime-scented, coconut-flavored bun with a dollop of pineapple preserves in the center. These are especially delicious with fresh, tropical fruit for brunch.

MAKES 6

1 cup (120 g) self-rising flour, plus more for work surface

1 cup (250 g) plain Greek yogurt

4 tbsp (50 g) sugar

2 tbsp (30 g) cold butter, grated

1 tsp coconut extract

1 tsp lime zest

1 egg, beaten

⅓ cup (110 g) pineapple preserves

2 tbsp (10 g) coconut, shredded

Preheat the oven to 425°F (220°C). Line a baking sheet with parchment paper.

In a medium bowl, combine the flour, yogurt, sugar, butter, coconut extract and lime zest. Stir until a shaggy dough forms.

Sprinkle flour onto a work surface. Turn out the dough onto the work surface and knead until the dough develops into a smooth ball, about 1 minute. Divide the dough into six separate segments. Roll each dough section into a ball and push your thumb through the middle, as if you were making a bagel.

Place the rolls on the prepared baking sheet and brush each one with the egg. Fill the center of the rolls with pineapple preserves and sprinkle with coconut. Bake the kolaches for 15 to 18 minutes, or until they are golden brown. Let the kolaches cool for 10 minutes and serve warm.

CARAMEL-APPLE KUCHEN

A kuchen is a German-style cake or pastry, generally used as an afternoon accompaniment to a cup of tea. This version is full of buttery, dark brown sugar–coated apples. Your house will smell amazing as the kuchen bakes. You could swap out the apples for plums, peaches or apricots, but you won't need to cook them in the microwave first if you do. Be sure to use apples that hold up well in baking. My favorites are Granny Smith, Golden Delicious or Honeycrisp.

SERVES 9

1 cup (120 g) self-rising flour

1 cup (250 g) vanilla-flavored Greek yogurt

2 tbsp (25 g) sugar

6 tbsp (90 ml) butter, melted, divided

2 apples, peeled, cored and thinly sliced

⅓ cup (80 ml) apple juice

1 cup (225 g) brown sugar, packed

1 tsp ground cinnamon

Powdered sugar, for serving

Preheat the oven to 425°F (220°C). Coat an 8- or 9-inch (20- or 23-cm) baking dish with butter or nonstick cooking spray.

In a large bowl, combine the flour, yogurt, sugar and 4 tablespoons (60 ml) melted butter. Stir until the dough is just combined, and press the dough into the prepared baking dish.

Place the apple slices in a medium microwaveable bowl. Add the apple juice. Microwave the apples on high for 2 minutes, or until just beginning to soften. Add the remaining 2 tablespoons (30 ml) of melted butter, brown sugar and cinnamon to the apples, stirring until combined.

Pour the apple mixture over the dough in the prepared baking dish. Bake for 24 to 26 minutes, or until the edges are browned and the middle springs back when touched. Let it cool for 10 minutes. Sprinkle with powdered sugar and serve immediately.

EASY LIEGE-STYLE WAFFLES
WITH BERRIES AND BELGIAN CHOCOLATE

I fell in love with Liege waffles on a trip to Belgium. These aren't the giant Saturday morning, syrup-coated breakfast waffles that we eat in America. These are smaller, irregularly shaped, buttery and sugary crisp waffles, topped with fruit and whipped cream, and even better, melted Belgian chocolate. These waffles are absolutely at their best right out of the waffle iron. If you need to make them a little bit early, just complete the waffle-making process, but then slip the prepared Liege waffles back onto the hot waffle maker to heat back up for a few minutes. If you don't want to fuss with berries and chocolate, you can also dip these in melted butter and coat them with a dusting of cinnamon and sugar.

MAKES 8 SMALL WAFFLES

1 cup (120 g) self-rising flour

1 cup (250 g) plain Greek yogurt

¼ cup (60 ml) butter, melted

½ cup (65 g) pearl sugar (see notes)

1 cup (160 g) strawberries, sliced, mixed with 1 tbsp (12 g) sugar, if desired

¼ cup (15 g) whipped cream, for serving

¼ cup (60 ml) Belgian chocolate, melted, or other high-quality chocolate, for serving

Preheat a standard waffle maker. In a large bowl, combine the flour, yogurt and butter with a wooden spoon until just combined.

Divide the dough into eight equal pieces and roll each piece into a ball. Roll each ball in 1 tablespoon (16 g) of the pearl sugar, pressing in slightly to get them to adhere. Cook the balls in the waffle iron until they are golden brown.

Serve each waffle with ⅛ cup (20 g) of strawberries, a ½ tablespoon (2 g) of whipped cream and a ½ tablespoon (8 ml) of chocolate.

NOTES: You can find pearl sugar at specialty stores or online through Amazon. If you can't wait for pearl sugar, just substitute coarsely crushed sugar cubes.

To make cleaning the waffle iron a little easier, just place a wet paper towel on the hot waffle iron surface and let it sit for 5 minutes. It should wipe clean very easily.

JUICY BLACKBERRY COBBLER

My sister asked me about my favorite two-ingredient dough recipe. While it's almost impossible for me to pick, this Juicy Blackberry Cobbler immediately came to mind. It's a little unusual in that you make the dough and spread it on the bottom of the pan and then top it with sugared berries that become syrupy and sticky, sinking into the dough. I could eat the whole pan for breakfast, lunch, dinner or dessert. It's even better with a little whipped cream or vanilla ice cream.

SERVES 9

2½ cups (365 g) blackberries, thawed if frozen

¾ cup plus 2 tbsp (175 g) sugar, divided

1 cup (120 g) self-rising flour

1 cup (250 g) plain Greek yogurt

¼ cup (60 ml) butter, melted

Combine the blackberries and ¾ cup (150 g) of sugar in a large bowl and let stand for about 20 minutes, or until the berries become syrupy.

Preheat the oven to 425°F (220°C). Coat an 8- or 9-inch (20- or 23-cm) square glass baking dish with butter or nonstick cooking spray.

In a medium bowl, combine the flour, yogurt, remaining 2 tablespoons (25 g) of sugar and butter using a wooden spoon. Spread the dough into the prepared baking dish.

Pour the berry mixture over the top and bake for 33 to 37 minutes, or until the edges are golden brown and the middle springs back when you touch it. Let it cool for 5 minutes. Serve warm if you can!

STRAWBERRY TWISTS
WITH LEMONADE DIPPING SAUCE

These are such a fun, portable treat, even on their own, but the lemonade dipping sauce makes them extra exciting. These have a triple zing of lemon from lemon extract, fresh lemon juice and lemon zest. If you want to vary the flavor, try using blackberry, raspberry, blueberry or mixed berry jam or preserves.

MAKES 8 TWISTS

TWISTS

1 cup (120 g) self-rising flour, plus more for work surface

1 cup (250 g) plain Greek yogurt

2 tbsp (30 g) cold butter, grated

4 tbsp (50 g) sugar, divided

½ tsp lemon extract

¼ cup (80 g) strawberry jam

1 egg, beaten

DIPPING SAUCE

1 cup (135 g) powdered sugar

4 tbsp (60 g) lemon juice

1 tsp lemon zest

Preheat the oven to 425°F (220°C). Line a baking sheet with parchment paper.

For the twists, in a medium bowl, combine the flour, yogurt, butter, 3 tablespoons (40 g) of sugar and lemon extract.

Generously flour a work surface. Transfer the dough to the work surface and knead a few times, just until the mixture develops into a smooth ball. Roll or pat the dough into a 12 x 8-inch (30 x 20-cm) rectangle. Spread the jam onto the dough and roll it up, as if you were making cinnamon rolls, starting with the long edge, forming a cylinder of dough. Cut the dough in half horizontally. You should have two cylinders of dough. Cut each cylinder lengthwise into four strips. You should have eight strips of dough.

Place the dough on the prepared parchment paper and twist a few times until each has a spiral shape that shows some of the jam. Brush the twists with the egg and sprinkle with the remaining tablespoon (10 g) of sugar.

Bake the twists for about 16 to 18 minutes, or until they are golden brown.

For the dipping sauce, combine the powdered sugar, lemon juice and lemon zest to form a smooth icing. Serve warm with big napkins for the drippy sauce.

STRAWBERRY SHORTCAKES WITH CREAM CHEESE FILLING

There's no better sunny celebration dessert than strawberry shortcake when the strawberries are ripe, sweet and juicy. I like to set up a make-your-own shortcake bar with sweetened strawberries—yes, but with lots of other fruit options as well. If you're feeling adventurous, try your next shortcake with strawberries, pineapple, mango and a little sprinkle of coconut and a squeeze of lime.

MAKES 4

SHORTCAKE

1 cup (120 g) self-rising flour, plus more for work surface

1 cup (250 g) plain Greek yogurt

2 tbsp (30 g) butter, cold, grated

6 tbsp (75 g) sugar, divided

1 egg, beaten

STRAWBERRIES

1 cup (160 g) strawberries, sliced, stems removed

1 tbsp (13 g) sugar

CREAM CHEESE FILLING

½ cup (120 ml) whipping cream

4 oz (115 g) cream cheese

½ tsp vanilla extract

2 tbsp (20 g) powdered sugar

Preheat the oven to 425°F (220°C). Line a baking sheet with parchment paper.

For the shortcakes, in a medium bowl, combine the flour, yogurt, butter and 4 tablespoons (50 g) of sugar.

Generously flour a work surface. Turn out the dough onto the work surface and knead a few times, just until the dough develops into a smooth ball. Divide the dough into four equal pieces. Shape each piece into a disk, about 3 inches (8 cm) in diameter. Place the four shortcakes on the prepared baking sheet, brush with egg and sprinkle with the remaining 2 tablespoons (25 g) of sugar. Bake for 16 to 18 minutes, or until they are golden brown.

For the strawberries, in a medium bowl, combine the strawberries and sugar and allow to sit while the shortcakes bake.

For the cream cheese filling, in a medium bowl, using a handheld mixer set to a high speed, whip the cream until soft peaks form. Add the cream cheese and continue to beat at high speed until the cream cheese is incorporated and the filling is light and airy. Add the vanilla and the powdered sugar and beat until combined.

To serve, slice the shortcakes in half horizontally. Layer the strawberries and cream cheese filling on the bottom half of the shortcakes and cover with a shortcake top. Serve immediately.

BROWN SUGAR AND OATMEAL STREUSEL-TOPPED BLUEBERRY MINICAKES

These little cakes are cousins of muffins, generous with lots of blueberries and a sweet and inviting topping made from buttery brown sugar and oats. I make these cakes in small batches for our family of four. You might want to double the recipe if you're baking for a crowd, or if you want to make some extra to pop in the freezer. If I do freeze these cakes, I freeze them in individual zip-top bags so that I can grab one out at a time to put in the kids' lunches for a sweet little treat. If you pull them out frozen in the morning, they'll be perfectly defrosted by lunchtime.

MAKES 6

CAKE

1 cup (120 g) self-rising flour

1 cup (250 g) vanilla-flavored Greek yogurt

1 egg

2 tbsp (30 ml) butter, melted

6 tbsp (75 g) granulated sugar

1 tsp vanilla extract

¾ cup (75 g) blueberries

STREUSEL

1½ tbsp (25 ml) butter, melted

5 tbsp (70 g) brown sugar

⅓ cup (30 g) quick-cooking or old-fashioned oats

Preheat the oven to 425°F (220°C). Lightly butter a six-cup-capacity muffin tin.

For the cake, in a medium bowl, combine the flour, yogurt, egg, melted butter, granulated sugar and vanilla, mixing well. Gently stir in the blueberries. Divide the dough between the six muffin cups, filling all the way to the top, since the muffins will only rise a little.

For the streusel, in a small bowl, combine the melted butter with the brown sugar and oats. Sprinkle over the tops of the muffin batter. Bake the muffins for about 18 minutes, or until puffed and golden brown. Let them cool for about 5 minutes, and then remove the muffins from the muffin pan. Serve warm with a little butter, if you like.

CRANBERRY AND LEMON HOT CROSS BUNS

It's an Easter family breakfast tradition to have hot cross buns before we start our Easter egg hunt. I used to spend hours getting the dough ready and waiting for it to rise, but now I wake up with the kids and bake these up, start to finish, in about 30 minutes, with no more than 10 minutes of prep time. They're every bit as delicious as the yeast-risen variety. I like to make them with dried cranberries, plumped up in boiling water.

MAKES 8

BUNS

½ cup (120 ml) boiling water

½ cup (60 g) dried cranberries or currants

1¼ cups (150 g) self-rising flour, plus more for work surface

1 cup (250 g) vanilla-flavored Greek yogurt

2 tbsp (30 ml) butter, melted

1 tbsp (10 g) lemon or orange zest

1 tsp ground cinnamon

1 egg

4 tbsp (50 g) granulated sugar

GLAZE

½ cup (70 g) powdered sugar

2 tsp (10 ml) milk or cream

¼ tsp vanilla extract

First things first. Pour the boiling water over the dried cranberries and set them aside while you prepare everything else.

Preheat the oven to 425°F (220°C). Line a baking sheet with parchment paper.

For the buns, in a medium bowl, combine the flour, yogurt, butter, lemon zest, cinnamon, egg and granulated sugar. Drain the cranberries of any excess liquid and stir them into the dough. Generously flour a work surface. Turn out the dough onto the work surface and knead for a few turns, just until the dough is a little less sticky and more manageable.

Cut the dough into eight equal pieces and roll each piece into a ball. Place the dough balls on the prepared baking sheet, spacing at least 2 inches (5 cm) apart. Bake for about 18 minutes, or until they are golden brown.

Remove them from the oven and allow to cool for 10 minutes.

For the glaze, in a small bowl, combine the powdered sugar, milk and vanilla into a thick, smooth mixture. Spoon the mixture into a zip-top bag. Snip off a corner of the bag, and pipe a cross or X on the top of each roll.

PEACH BEEHIVES WITH HONEY BUTTER

For me, summer starts with the first bite of a perfect, golden peach. I make it a point to eat one daily until the season is over, and that means it's time for autumn. I buy extra peaches to make this adorable little dessert. The peaches are wrapped in strips of pastry and baked in a little bundle that resembles a beehive, then topped with a creamy, sweet dollop of honey butter. You don't need to peel or pit the peaches. The skin will almost melt away in the baking, and the pit can easily be removed with a spoon while you are eating your dessert.

MAKES 4

1 cup (120 g) self-rising flour, plus more for work surface

1 cup (250 g) plain Greek yogurt

¼ tsp nutmeg

4 whole small peaches, washed and dried, unpeeled and unpitted

1 egg, beaten

3 tbsp (40 g) butter, softened

2 tbsp (30 ml) honey

½ tsp vanilla extract

Preheat the oven to 350°F (180°C). Lightly grease an 8 x 8-inch (20 x 20-cm) baking dish.

In a large bowl, combine the flour, yogurt and nutmeg, mixing with a wooden spoon just until a sticky dough forms.

Generously flour a work surface and turn out the dough onto the surface. Knead the dough a few times, sprinkling with more flour as needed, until the dough is no longer sticky. Roll or press the dough into a rectangle, about 12 x 10 inches (30 x 25 cm). Don't be too picky about the shape. Cut the dough into ½-inch (1.3-cm) long strips.

Hold a peach, stem side down, and wrap it in a dough strip, overlapping the dough and pinching the seams to seal. Be sure the peach is completely covered in dough. Repeat the process with all the peaches and then place them into the baking dish. Brush each peach with the beaten egg.

Bake for 35 to 40 minutes. If the dough begins to brown before 35 minutes of baking, cover with foil, but continue to bake to be sure the peaches are completely cooked through.

Meanwhile, in a medium bowl, combine the butter, honey and vanilla, beating until it becomes light and fluffy. Let the beehives cool for 10 minutes in the baking dish. Transfer the beehives to a platter and cover each one with a big dollop of honey butter to melt over the top of each one.

ORANGE CREAMSICLE LOAF CAKE

I almost want to call this a creamsicle pound cake, since with its velvety texture and tight crumb, it sure seems like one! This cake starts with the basic formula for two-ingredient dough—yogurt and self-rising flour—but quickly transforms into a fun twist on that summertime orange and vanilla ice-cream popsicle. The cake itself is flavored with orange extract—don't substitute orange juice, since it won't be potent enough. If you can't find orange extract, use thawed frozen orange juice concentrate, but increase the quantity to ¼ cup (60 ml).

SERVES 8

CAKE

1 cup (120 g) self-rising flour

1 cup (250 g) plain Greek yogurt

½ cup (120 ml) butter, melted

1 cup (195 g) granulated sugar

2 eggs

Zest of 1 orange

1 tbsp (15 ml) orange extract

GLAZE

1½ cups (200 g) powdered sugar

1 tsp vanilla extract

3 tbsp (45 ml) cream

Preheat the oven to 350°F (180°C). Grease an 8- or 9-inch (20- or 23-cm) loaf pan.

For the cake, in a large bowl, gently combine the flour, yogurt, butter, granulated sugar, eggs, orange zest and orange extract with a rubber spatula until it's well combined. Pour the batter into the greased loaf pan. Bake for 30 minutes, then tent it with foil and bake for about another 15 minutes, or until a toothpick inserted into the center comes out clean.

Let the cake cool in the loaf pan for 10 minutes before removing from the pan. Transfer the cake to a plate to cool completely.

For the glaze, in a medium bowl, combine the powdered sugar, vanilla and cream, beating until it's smooth and creamy. Frost the cooled cake with the glaze.

GINGER AND BROWN SUGAR BANANA CAKE

If you don't have an overripe banana for this cake, just put a fresh banana on a baking sheet and place it in the oven while the oven preheats. When the skin on the baked banana is blackened, it's ready to use in this recipe. I also like to freeze overripe bananas, cut into 1-inch (2.5-cm) pieces, so they're ready to thaw and use in banana cake at any time. My banana cake is rich with caramel undertones from the dark brown sugar and just a little hint of ginger. You could bake this as a traditional banana bread loaf, but I like to bake it as a cake so there is more surface area for the brown sugar topping. I always make this cake when we have overnight guests, since it works well for a snack, dessert—with cinnamon ice cream—or even breakfast treat.

SERVES 9

1 overripe banana

1 cup (250 g) plain Greek yogurt

2 eggs

⅓ cup (80 ml) vegetable oil

1 tsp vanilla extract

1¼ cups (285 g) dark brown sugar, divided

½ tsp ground cinnamon, plus more for the top

½ tsp dried ginger

1 cup (120 g) self-rising flour

¾ cup (90 g) walnuts, chopped and toasted, optional

Preheat the oven to 350°F (180°C). Lightly grease an 8 x 8-inch (20 x 20-cm) baking dish.

In a large bowl, mash the banana with a fork until it is almost smooth. Add the yogurt, eggs, oil, vanilla and 1 cup (225 g) of brown sugar, mixing until smooth, about 1 minute. Gently stir in the cinnamon, ginger and flour, stirring just until combined. Add the walnuts now, if you are using them.

Pour the batter into the prepared baking dish. Sprinkle the top of the cake the with remaining ¼ cup (60 g) of brown sugar. Sprinkle a little bit of cinnamon on top of the cake. Bake for 35 to 40 minutes, or until the center springs back when touched lightly. Let it cool for 5 minutes.

NOTE: The cake is delicious warm out of the oven, but it might even be better the next day when the flavors have had a chance to develop.

FUDGY DOUBLE CHOCOLATE SNACK CAKE

This is the one and only chocolate recipe in this cookbook. I adore chocolate, but I wanted to make sure I created something really special if I was going to include it. It's fitting that I put it last, since it's a very nice note to end on. This is classic enough for an everyday, after-school kind of cake, but it's also fancy enough for company—especially if you dress up it with a dusting of powdered sugar and a smattering of fresh raspberries. You can also add some frosting and sprinkles, if you're trying to win over some of the young at heart. On a final note, if you hit the preheat button on your oven, you can have everything stirred up and ready to go before the oven gets to 350°F (180°C).

SERVES 9

1 cup (120 g) self-rising flour

1 cup (250 g) plain Greek yogurt

½ cup (60 g) cocoa powder

½ cup (120 ml) butter, melted

1 cup (195 g) sugar

1 tsp vanilla extract

2 eggs

¾ cup (140 g) milk chocolate or semisweet chocolate chips, tossed with 2 tbsp (15 g) flour

½ cup (65 g) toasted pecans, chopped, optional

1 cup chocolate frosting, homemade or store-bought, optional

Sprinkles, optional

Preheat the oven to 350°F (180°C). Grease an 8- or 9-inch (20- or 23-cm) loaf pan with butter, or coat with nonstick cooking spray.

In a large bowl, combine the flour, yogurt, cocoa, butter, sugar, vanilla and eggs. Stir just until the mixture comes together into a smooth batter. Add the chocolate chips and the pecans, if using. Pour into the prepared baking pan.

Bake for 32 to 36 minutes, or until the middle springs back when lightly pressed. Let the cake cool for 10 minutes before serving, or let it cool completely and frost with chocolate frosting and top with sprinkles.

ACKNOWLEDGMENTS

Who can know what it takes to write a cookbook? I didn't, but there were a few people who did, and they helped me figure it out.

To Brooke Lark, who made it seem like the easiest thing to pitch an idea to a publisher and make it happen.

To Elizabeth Seise and Marissa Giambelluca at Page Street Publishing, who not only said yes to an idea but answered all of my questions, and kept the project moving along.

To my editor, Darya Crockett, who patiently dotted all the figurative i's and crossed all the figurative t's that I had neglected, and there were more than a few.

To Ken Goodman, whose expertise in the kitchen and behind the camera made the book into a beautiful reality.

And to those who have no idea what it takes to write a cookbook, but listened to me talk about it almost incessantly and now know much more than they ever, ever wanted to know.

To my family, Sailor, West and Shane, for offering compliments and constructive criticism in equal measure, but most of all, for letting my cookbook become a family project.

To my parents, who never stop being enthusiastic for whatever I'm throwing myself into.

To my sisters, my secret source of confidence, who constantly convince me that I can do it, whatever "it" happens to be. And to my brothers, for encouraging me to make a one-ingredient cookbook (ha!) on my next go-around.

To my Instagram family, for showing up with a smile every day. Your comments and messages make every day a little brighter.

Thank you isn't big enough. I just don't see how I could have done this without your unfailing support. All my love and gratitude.

—Erin

ABOUT THE AUTHOR

ERIN RENOUF MYLROIE is a humanities professor and mentor by day, and a recipe developer and Instagrammer by night. Her passions include travel, poetry, crossword puzzles, fitness, healthy meals, decadent treats and, of course, two-ingredient miracle dough. Erin has shared her award-winning recipes on the Food Network, the *Rachael Ray* show and *Studio Five*, where she is a regular contributor, as well as in several publications, such as *Better Homes and Gardens*, *Bon Appetit*, *Cooking Light*, and *Woman's Day* magazine. She lives in Southern Utah with her husband and two children.

INDEX

A

apples, in Caramel-Apple Kuchen, 148

artichokes, in Four Seasons Sheet Pan Pizza—Pizza Quattro Stagioni, 81

Avocado, California Pizza with Fresh Greens, Olives and, 77

Avocado and Frizzled Egg Flatbreads, Super-Food Crispy Kale, 69

B

Bacon, Fig and Gruyère Volcano Rolls, 58

bagels

  Basic Bagels with Master Recipe, 10

  Cinnamon-Raisin-Walnut Bagels with Honey-Walnut Cream Cheese, 17

  Double Everything Bagels, 14

  French Toast Cinnamon and Maple Bites, 132

  Garlic and Cheddar Bagel Twists, 18

  Israeli Sesame Ring Bread with Salt and Herbs for Dipping, 29

  Sun-Dried Tomato Pesto Cream Cheese–Stuffed Bagel Balls, 22

  Triple Onion Cream Cheese–Stuffed Bagel Balls, 21

Banana Cake, Ginger and Brown Sugar, 167

Barbecue Chicken, Chinese Bao with Plum, 98

Basic Bagels with Master Recipe, 10

beef

  Chilean-Style Cumin-Scented Beef Empanadas, 105

  English Beef and Potato Hand Pie "Pasties," 113

  Philadelphia Cheesesteak Stromboli, 94

Biscuits, Cheddar and Old Bay Butter-Topped Drop, 37

Biscuits, Monterey Jack Cheese, Dill and Scallion, 34

Black Bean and Pepper Jack Baked Huevos Rancheros, 74

Blackberry Cobbler, Juicy, 152

Blueberry Minicakes, Brown Sugar and Oatmeal Streusel-Topped, 159

Blueberry-Lemon Visiting Loaf, 135

bratwurst, in Octoberfest Cheesy Mustard-Wrapped Brats, 117

breads

  Blueberry-Lemon Visiting Loaf, 135
  Caramelized Onion, Asiago and Rosemary Focaccia, 62

  Cheddar, Onion and Black Pepper Visiting Loaf, 25

  Cinnamon-Cardamom Braid, 128

  Irish Dilly-Rye Loaf, 42

  Pesto-Parmesan Twists, 46

  Pita Pockets with Cucumber Raita, 26

  Red Onion and Gruyère Fougasse, 33

  Rustic Olive, Feta and Roasted Red Pepper Loaf, 30

  Strawberry Twists with Lemonade Dipping Sauce, 155

  Sweet Irish Soda Bread with Currants and Raisins, 144

Brown Sugar and Oatmeal Streusel-Topped Blueberry Minicakes, 159

Buffalo Chicken and Blue Cheese Pockets, 106

Buns, Maple-Pecan Sticky, 127

Buns, Poppy Seed Hamburger, 38

Butternut Squash Potpie with Sage-Herbed Crust, Chicken and, 97

Buttery Honey Dijon–Glazed Soft Pretzels, 50

Buttery Parmesan and Garlic Knots, 57

C

cakes

  Brown Sugar and Oatmeal Streusel-Topped Blueberry Minicakes, 159

  Caramel-Apple Kuchen, 148

  Fudgy Double Chocolate Snack Cake, 168

  Ginger and Brown Sugar Banana Cake, 167

  Orange Creamsicle Loaf Cake, 164

  Strawberry Shortcakes with Cream Cheese Filling, 156

California Pizza with Fresh Greens, Olives and Avocado, 77

Calzones, Spicy Italian Sausage and Mozzarella, 70

Caramel-Apple Kuchen, 148

Caramelized Onion, Asiago and Rosemary Focaccia, 62

Cheddar and Old Bay Butter-Topped Drop Biscuits, 37

cheese

  Bacon, Fig and Gruyère Volcano Rolls, 58

  Black Bean and Pepper Jack Baked Huevos Rancheros, 74

  Buffalo Chicken and Blue Cheese Pockets, 106

  Buttery Parmesan and Garlic Knots, 57

  Caramelized Onion, Asiago and Rosemary Focaccia, 62

  Cheddar, Onion and Black Pepper Visiting Loaf, 25

  Cheddar and Old Bay Butter-Topped Drop Biscuits, 37

  Cinnamon-Raisin-Walnut Bagels with Honey-Walnut Cream Cheese, 17

Denver Ham and Cheddar Breakfast Pockets, 73

Garlic and Cheddar Bagel Twists, 18

Georgian Cheese and Egg Bread—Khachapuri, 110

Giant Cream Cheese and Jalapeño-Stuffed Pretzel for a Crowd, 54

Lemon Cream Cheese Breakfast Pastries, 131

Maple Bacon, Jalapeño and Gruyère Good Morning Flatbreads, 66

Monterey Jack Cheese, Dill and Scallion Biscuits, 34

Octoberfest Cheesy Mustard-Wrapped Brats, 117

Pesto-Parmesan Twists, 46

Philadelphia Cheesesteak Stromboli, 94

Pizza Bianco–Style Fig, Prosciutto and Cheese Sandwich, 114

Pretzels Bites with Sweet and Tangy Cheese Sauce, 53

Red Onion and Gruyère Fougasse, 33

Rustic Olive, Feta and Roasted Red Pepper Loaf, 30

Spicy Italian Sausage and Mozzarella Calzones, 70

Spicy Pepper Jack Jalapeño Roll-Ups, 49

Spinach, Feta and Red Bell Pepper Breakfast Flatbreads, 65

Spinach, Gruyère and Bacon Quiche, 121

Strawberry Shortcakes with Cream Cheese Filling, 156

Sun-Dried Tomato Pesto Cream Cheese–Stuffed Bagel Balls, 22

Three-Cheese Empanadas, 102

Triple Onion Cream Cheese–Stuffed Bagel Balls, 21

chicken

Buffalo Chicken and Blue Cheese Pockets, 106

Chicken and Butternut Squash Potpie with Sage-Herbed Crust, 97

Chinese Bao with Plum Barbecue Chicken, 98

Grilled Moroccan Chicken and Vegetable Flatbread, 109

Chilean-Style Cumin-Scented Beef Empanadas, 105

Chinese Bao with Plum Barbecue Chicken, 98

chocolate

Cini-Mini Churros with Milk Chocolate Dipping Sauce, 139

Easy Liege-Style Waffles with Berries and Belgian Chocolate, 151

Fudgy Double Chocolate Snack Cake, 168

Chorizo and Pickled Jalapeño Kolaches, Texas, 118

Cini-Mini Churros with Milk Chocolate Dipping Sauce, 139

Cinnamon-Cardamom Braid, 128

Cinnamon-Raisin-Walnut Bagels with Honey-Walnut Cream Cheese, 17

Classic Sausage and Pepperoni Stromboli, 93

Cobbler, Juicy Blackberry, 152

Coconut Kolaches, Pineapple and, 147

Coffee Cake, New York–Style Crumb, 136

Cranberry and Lemon Hot Cross Buns, 160

Cucumber Raita, Pita Pockets with, 26

Currants and Raisins, Sweet Irish Soda Bread with, 144

Curried Potato and Pea Samosas, 101

D

Deep-Dish Chicago-Style Pizza, 82

Denver Ham and Cheddar Breakfast Pockets, 73

Dijon–Glazed Soft Pretzels, Buttery Honey, 50

Donut Holes, Raspberry-Filled Jelly, 143

Donuts—Castagnole, Lemon and Vanilla Italian, 140

Double Everything Bagels, 14

E

Easy Liege-Style Waffles with Berries and Belgian Chocolate, 151

eggs

Black Bean and Pepper Jack Baked Huevos Rancheros, 74

Georgian Cheese and Egg Bread—Khachapuri, 110

Spinach, Gruyère and Bacon Quiche, 121

Super-Food Crispy Kale, Avocado and Frizzled Egg Flatbreads, 69

Empanadas, Chilean-Style Cumin-Scented Beef, 105

Empanadas, Three-Cheese, 102

English Beef and Potato Hand Pie "Pasties," 113

Everything Bagel Seasoning, 14

F

flatbreads

Grilled Moroccan Chicken and Vegetable Flatbread, 109

Maple Bacon, Jalapeño and Gruyère Good Morning Flatbreads, 66

Spinach, Feta and Red Bell Pepper Breakfast Flatbreads, 65

Super-Food Crispy Kale, Avocado and Frizzled Egg Flatbreads, 69

Focaccia, Caramelized Onion, Asiago and Rosemary, 62

Four Seasons Sheet Pan Pizza—Pizza Quattro Stagioni, 81

French Toast Cinnamon and Maple Bites, 132

Fudgy Double Chocolate Snack Cake, 168

G

Garlic and Cheddar Bagel Twists, 18

Georgian Cheese and Egg Bread—
Khachapuri, 110

German Seeded Rye Rolls, 41

Giant Cream Cheese and Jalapeño-
Stuffed Pretzel for a Crowd, 54

Ginger and Brown Sugar Banana Cake,
167

Golden Potato and Rosemary Pizza, 85

Grandma's Long Island Tomato and Herb
Pizza, 78

Grilled Moroccan Chicken and Vegetable
Flatbread, 109

H

Ham and Cheddar Breakfast Pockets,
Denver, 73

Hand Pie "Pasties," English Beef and
Potato, 113

Hot Cross Buns, Cranberry and Lemon,
160

Huevos Rancheros, Black Bean and
Pepper Jack Baked, 74

I

Irish Dilly-Rye Loaf, 42

Israeli Sesame Ring Bread with Salt and
Herbs for Dipping, 29

J

jalapeños
   Giant Cream Cheese and Jalapeño-
   Stuffed Pretzel for a Crowd, 54
   Maple Bacon, Jalapeño and Gruyère
   Good Morning Flatbreads, 66
   Spicy Pepper Jack Jalapeño Roll-
   Ups, 49
   Texas Chorizo and Pickled Jalapeño
   Kolaches, 118

Juicy Blackberry Cobbler, 152

K

Kale, Avocado and Frizzled Egg
Flatbreads, Super-Food Crispy, 69

Kolaches, Pineapple and Coconut, 147

Kolaches, Texas Chorizo and Pickled
Jalapeño, 118

Kuchen, Caramel-Apple, 148

L

Lemon and Vanilla Italian Donuts—
Castagnole, 140

Lemon Cream Cheese Breakfast
Pastries, 131

Lemon Hot Cross Buns, Cranberry and,
160

M

Make Your Own Self-Rising Flour, 11

Maple Bacon, Jalapeño and Gruyère Good
Morning Flatbreads, 66

Maple-Pecan Sticky Buns, 127

Master Recipe, Basic Bagels with, 10

Monterey Jack Cheese, Dill and Scallion
Biscuits, 34

mushrooms
   Classic Sausage and Pepperoni
   Stromboli, 93
   Deep-Dish Chicago-Style Pizza, 82
   Four Seasons Sheet Pan Pizza—Pizza
   Quattro Stagioni, 81
   Philadelphia Cheesesteak Stromboli, 94

N

New York–Style Crumb Coffee Cake, 136

O

Octoberfest Cheesy Mustard-Wrapped
Brats, 117

Olive, Feta and Roasted Red Pepper Loaf,
Rustic, 30

Olive and Caper Pissaladière, Southern
French, 90

Olive Oil, Tomato and Herb Pizza al
Capriccio, 89

Olives and Avocado, California Pizza with
Fresh Greens, 77

Orange Creamsicle Loaf Cake, 164

oranges, in Raspberry-Orange Breakfast
Rolls, 124

P

Pastries, Lemon Cream Cheese
Breakfast, 131

Pea Samosas, Curried Potato and, 101

Peach Beehives with Honey Butter, 163

pecans, in Maple-Pecan Sticky Buns, 127

Pepperoni Stromboli, Classic Sausage
and, 93

Pesto-Parmesan Twists, 46

Philadelphia Cheesesteak Stromboli, 94

Pineapple and Coconut Kolaches, 147

Pita Pockets with Cucumber Raita, 26

pizzas
   California Pizza with Fresh Greens,
   Olives and Avocado, 77
   Deep-Dish Chicago-Style Pizza, 82
   Four Seasons Sheet Pan Pizza—Pizza
   Quattro Stagioni, 81
   Golden Potato and Rosemary Pizza, 85
   Grandma's Long Island Tomato and
   Herb Pizza, 78
   Olive Oil, Tomato and Herb Pizza al
   Capriccio, 89
   Pizza Bianco–Style Fig, Prosciutto and
   Cheese Sandwich, 114
   Southern French Olive and Caper
   Pissaladière, 90
   30-Minute Start-to-Finish Pizza
   Margherita, 86

Poppy Seed Hamburger Buns, 38

Potato and Pea Samosas, Curried, 101

Potato and Rosemary Pizza, Golden, 85

Potato Hand Pie "Pasties," English Beef and, 113

Potpie with Sage Herbed Crust, Chicken and Butternut Squash, 97

pretzels

    Buttery Honey Dijon–Glazed Soft Pretzels, 50

    Giant Cream Cheese and Jalapeño-Stuffed Pretzel for a Crowd, 54

    Pretzels Bites with Sweet and Tangy Cheese Sauce, 53

Prosciutto and Cheese Sandwich, Pizza Bianco–Style Fig, 114

Q

Quiche, Spinach, Gruyère and Bacon, 121

R

Raspberry-Filled Jelly Donut Holes, 143

Raspberry-Orange Breakfast Rolls, 124

Red Onion and Gruyère Fougasse, 33

Red Pepper Loaf, Rustic Olive, Feta and Roasted, 30

rolls

    Bacon, Fig and Gruyère Volcano Rolls, 58

    Buttery Parmesan and Garlic Knots, 57

    German Seeded Rye Rolls, 41

    Peach Beehives with Honey Butter, 163

    Raspberry-Orange Breakfast Rolls, 124

    Soft and Buttery Dinner Rolls, 45

    Spicy Pepper Jack Jalapeño Roll-Ups, 49

Rustic Olive, Feta and Roasted Red Pepper Loaf, 30

S

Samosas, Curried Potato and Pea, 101

sausage

    Classic Sausage and Pepperoni Stromboli, 93

    Octoberfest Cheesy Mustard-Wrapped Brats, 117

    Spicy Italian Sausage and Mozzarella Calzones, 70

    Texas Chorizo and Pickled Jalapeño Kolaches, 118

self-rising flours

    Make Your Own Self-Rising Flour, 11

    Rye Self-Rising Flour, 42

    Self-Rising Rye Wheat Flour Blend, 41

    Whole-Wheat Self-Rising Flour, 69

Soft and Buttery Dinner Rolls, 45

Southern French Olive and Caper Pissaladière, 90

Spicy Italian Sausage and Mozzarella Calzones, 70

Spicy Pepper Jack Jalapeño Roll-Ups, 49

Spinach, Feta and Red Bell Pepper Breakfast Flatbreads, 65

Spinach, Gruyère and Bacon Quiche, 121

Sticky Buns, Maple-Pecan, 127

Strawberry Shortcakes with Cream Cheese Filling, 156

Strawberry Twists with Lemonade Dipping Sauce, 155

Stromboli, Classic Sausage and Pepperoni, 93

Stromboli, Philadelphia Cheesesteak, 94

Sun-Dried Tomato Pesto Cream Cheese–Stuffed Bagel Balls, 22

Super-Food Crispy Kale, Avocado and Frizzled Egg Flatbreads, 69

Sweet Irish Soda Bread with Currants and Raisins, 144

T

Texas Chorizo and Pickled Jalapeño Kolaches, 118

30-Minute Start-to-Finish Pizza Margherita, 86

Three-Cheese Empanadas, 102

Tomato and Herb Pizza, Grandma's Long Island, 78

Tomato and Herb Pizza al Capriccio, Olive Oil, 89

Tomato Pesto Cream Cheese–Stuffed Bagel Balls, Sun-Dried, 22

Triple Onion Cream Cheese–Stuffed Bagel Balls, 21

W

Waffles with Berries and Belgian Chocolate, Easy Liege-Style, 151

walnuts, in Cinnamon-Raisin-Walnut Bagels with Honey-Walnut Cream Cheese, 17

Whole-Wheat Self-Rising Flour, 69